AMERICAN NEUTRALITY

Trial and Failure

BY

CHARLES G. FENWICK

GREENWOOD PRESS, PUBLISHERS
WESTPORT, CONNECTICUT

Library of Congress Cataloging in Publication Data

Fenwick, Charles Ghequiere, 1880-1973.
　　American neutrality, trial and failure.

　　Reprint of the 1940 ed. published by the New York
University Press, New York, issued in series:　James
Stokes lectureship on politics.
　　Includes index.
　　1. United States--Neutrality.　I.　Title.
II.　Series:　New York University.　Stokes Foundation.
James Stokes lectureship on politics.
JX1416.F4　1974　　　341.6'4　　　78-138609
ISBN 0-8371-5719-6

Originally published in 1940 by New York University Press,
New York and Oxford University Press, London

Reprinted in 1974 by Greenwood Press,
a division of Williamhouse-Regency Inc.

Library of Congress Catalog Card Number 78-138609

ISBN 0-8371-5719-6

Printed in the United States of America

James Stokes Lectureship on Politics
New York University · Stokes Foundation

AMERICAN NEUTRALITY
TRIAL AND FAILURE

PREFATORY NOTE

During the critical events of the past five years a majority of the American people have placed their faith in a policy of neutrality. Let war come in Europe, if it must; the United States would be neutral. Not only was the policy said to be justified by expediency, but it had sound national tradition behind it as well. By international law the neutral state had only to fulfill faithfully certain duties of neutrality and it could rest assured that its rights would be respected and it could remain at peace while the belligerents fought out their battles upon another continent. Whenever we had departed from that policy we had done so to our misfortune. If now we told the world our purpose to remain neutral and sought to forestall every danger of involvement, we could safely let events take their course without our interference.

The purpose of the author in preparing these lectures was to show the falsity of these assumptions—that neutrality, instead of being the simple formula it was believed to be, was an inherently illogical and paradoxical system which had neither the facts of history to justify it nor the logic of practical politics; that it led inevitably to the situation where the neutral must surrender certain rights not worth fighting for and prepare to defend others which were too vital to surrender. Moreover, the announcement in time of peace that the United States proposed to treat alike the law-breaker and his victim was, if not an invitation to lawlessness, certainly no deterrent to those who were prepared to resort to force to attain their objectives. Thus, while reliance upon neutrality had its appeal as an easy way of escape from the moral obligation to distinguish between right and wrong in the complex problems of international relations, it involved the great danger that adequate preparation would not be made to defend ourselves against the unpredictable outcome of the war in which it was proposed to be neutral no matter what issues might be at stake.

The manuscript of the volume was on its way to the press when the tragic events in Holland and Belgium took place which have caused such a profound change in American public opinion. It is believed, however, that the analysis of neutrality given in these pages is all the more effective because it was written in advance of these events and yet finds in them its fulfillment. The day of neutrality seems about to pass, whatever other day may come in its place.

My thanks are due to Dean Marshall S. Brown for his courtesy and cooperation in adjusting the dates of the lectures to suit my convenience when public duties made it impossible to keep to the dates originally fixed; and particularly am I indebted to my friend, Professor Clyde Eagleton, not only for reading the proofs and filling in references but for encouraging me in the belief that the interpretation of neutrality here given is fundamentally sound.

C. G. Fenwick

Rio de Janeiro
June 15, 1940

TABLE OF CONTENTS

AMERICAN NEUTRALITY
TRIAL AND FAILURE

I. INTRODUCTION

A few short years ago in the United States the word "neutrality" was one to conjure with. Many people used the phrase "neutrality for the United States" as if it had a sort of magical value, as if it were only necessary for the ship of state to set its course in the direction of true and tried "neutrality" and it would be possible to escape the storms with which other nations less wise were threatened. Neutrality even became with some persons an end in itself, as if it had a moral quality of its own; one had only to be neutral and peace was assured. Neutrality was readily identified with the policy of isolation. If there were threats of war abroad it was only necessary to continue repeating to the American public the formula: "Keep out, keep out," and all would be well. Other nations could have their wars if they wanted them; we would follow the counsels of the Founding Fathers and stay neutral.

It was a simple formula, this cult of neutrality, and it made its special appeal to those who had no faith in plans for leagues of nations and other forms of "collective security" by which certain misguided persons sought to lure the United States from its traditional detachment from the quarrels of other nations. To the "isolationists" such efforts to maintain international law and order by a system of cooperative defense were dangerous, almost provocative of war. There was no feasible way of distinguishing between right and wrong in the conflicts of nations; hence the simplest and safest plan was to keep out

Neutrality and isolation

1

*Difficul-
ties of
neutrality*

of it all, to be neutral. We made the mistake once of going to war to put an end to war; let that be enough.[1]

To say that the outbreak of the present war and the difficulties attending the lot of the neutral have completely shaken the faith of those who trusted in neutrality would scarcely be justified. But there is no doubt that there has been great disillusionment. At this time of writing the American people in large majority are still determined to keep out of the war, but their belief in the formula of neutrality as a means to that end is rapidly waning. They have come to see that in spite of their desire to be neutral, as they understood the word, they have been led inevitably to take sides in their sentiments between the belligerents, and they have found that it has not been easy to take sides in sentiment, to wish for the success of one of the belligerents, and at the same time to maintain an attitude of impartiality in the practical aspects of their conduct. They find themselves, therefore, embarrassed to insist upon their neutral rights when it means enforcing them against one whom they do not wish to see defeated; and they are beginning to

[1] There have been few more deceptive half-truths, repeated almost daily on the platform and in the press, than the statement that the .United States entered the World War in order to "end war," to "make the world safe for democracy," and otherwise to bring about a millennium. The immediate object of our declaration of war was specifically the redress of violations of our neutral rights. It took those violations to make us realize that our own national interest was involved in the defeat of the nation that was guilty of them. With that realization we then sought to give to the war a larger meaning than the mere redress of the violations of our neutral rights. So drastic is the nature of war and so heavy the price which even the victor must pay for his victory, that it would be strange if a nation that resorted to war did not seek something more from it than redress of the specific grievances that led to it. Why not prevent the conditions which gave rise to the war from recurring again? That would make the sacrifices better worth while. It is to the credit of American public opinion that this appeal to moral ideals came to take a larger place in its attitude towards the war than did the mere redress of wrongs done.

realize that those who argued the case of neutrality so effectively when war was merely an abstract proposition failed to take account of the one vital question—could one really be indifferent when certain fundamental principles of right or wrong were at issue? [2]

Slowly but surely the American public appears to be coming to understand that neutrality is not the simple thing it seemed to be; rather that it is an inherently illogical and inconsistent attitude, that it puts you in the position where you have to choose between abandoning your rights or fighting to maintain them. The latter course must obviously be ruled out in all but the gravest cases of violations of neutral right. For it would be the supreme folly to go to war to maintain your right to stay out of war. But the alternative of abandoning one's neutral rights as the price of peace is not so easy either. If the abandonment merely meant making a sacrifice for the sake of peace, the matter might end there. But the neutral may soon find that the abandonment of neutral rights raises a question of neutrality itself. The belligerent which suffers by the failure of the neutral to enforce its rights may threaten to regard the act

[2] This is the outstanding criticism that must be made of so many of the "volumes of disillusionment" that have appeared of recent years; e.g., Walter Millis, *Road to War; America 1914-1917* (1935); Charles C. Tansill, *America Goes to War* (1938), and others. The propagandists, whose evil deeds have been so graphically described, may have done a good job from 1914 to 1917; but it was not on false presentations of the facts that the American public made up its mind. From the day of the declaration of war the people of the United States began to take sides. Doubtless from the start a majority wanted the Allies to win. Slowly, with the violations of our neutral rights, that desire to have the Allies win developed into a realization that the United States had a vital national interest in the defeat of Germany. Without those violations to provoke us, our desire to have the Allies win might, for all the propaganda of parties financially interested, have gone no further than mere desire. Americans will take sides between belligerents as long as they can think for themselves. All the propagandists can do is to give them new reasons for doing what they have already made up their minds to do.

as a violation of neutral duty, so that the neutral is caught between the two horns of the dilemma. The fact that the United States is sufficiently powerful to be able to pursue the course which it believes to be correct without fear of being held to account by one or other of the belligerents may make its position easier in practice but does not dispose of the legal contradictions.[3] The troubles of a neutral are indeed many [4] as we shall see in detail later; and it is poor comfort to be told that there is no help for it so long as other nations choose to go to war. The American public, however, does not appear ready as yet to challenge their "right" to do so.

Neutrality an insecure basis of peace

The story of American neutrality is the story of a nation trying to live its own life in peace in the midst of lawlessness and anarchy. In the infancy of our Republic the task was a difficult one. We proclaimed a policy of political isolation, but saw no reason for adopting a similar policy of commercial isolation, and little by little we were drawn into the conflict. As we grew stronger and were able to defend ourselves against extravagant belligerent claims, it so happened that there was no major war in which to test our neutral position. Wars in remote sections, such as the Crimea, the Transvaal, and the Far East raised no acute issues of neutral right and neutral duty. Then came the World War and we found ourselves commercially entangled and emotionally aroused. Neutrality broke down in 1917 from its own inherent weaknesses and self-contradictions. For a brief

[3] Many persons fail to realize that it is not "neutrality" that makes it possible for the United States to keep out of war, but merely the strength of its armed forces. Reliance upon the "law" of neutrality alone would no more protect us than it has protected Norway or Denmark. All that the law of neutrality can do, even where its rules are clear, is to reduce controversies with countries that recognize the law. It is useless against the lawless.

[4] Charles Warren, in an article, "Troubles of a Neutral," *Foreign Affairs,* April, 1934, pp. 377-394, well described them, and his forecast has been fully borne out.

period at the close of the war we responded to the ideal of a system of cooperative defense which undertook to repudiate the principle itself of neutrality. Then once more, with the rejection of the Covenant of the League of Nations, neutrality reasserted itself; and now, twenty years later, with the outbreak of the present war, the inconsistencies and paradoxes of neutrality are again causing us embarrassment and making us realize how insecure is a peace that is built upon it.

To forecast the future of neutrality would be beyond our immediate task. The international scene is changing rapidly and new conditions are arising which must soon outdate judgments based upon the facts now before us. But it would at least seem clear that neutrality as it has been known in the past, the so-called "international law of neutrality," can scarcely survive the present war. Not even during the World War were such inroads made, as in the first six months of this war, upon principles thought to be solidly established. Whether the further progress of the war will result in a determination on the part of the American people to isolate and insulate themselves still further from a lawless world, to create an "Armed Neutrality" possibly of the whole western hemisphere, or in a conviction that the only hope for the future lies in the creation of a new and stronger international organization with the will and the power to do what the League of Nations failed to do, is a question which will doubtless only be answered as the war widens in range and develops in intensity. The lesson of the failure of traditional neutrality can scarcely be lost upon those who have tried that remedy and found it wanting.

The future of neutrality

II. THE DEVELOPMENT OF THE LAW
OF NEUTRALITY

Neutrality may be broadly defined as the attitude of a state
in remaining aloof from a war between two states or groups of
states, while maintaining towards them certain rights and ob-
serving certain duties defined by customary law and by international conventions or treaties. It is in point of law a special
status, with its own set of rights and duties qualifying the
normal rights and duties of states in time of peace. Let a war
start and whether the neutral likes it or not a new legal situation is created for it, which it has no choice but to accept. It
can go into the war if it likes; but if it decides to stay out it
must conform to a code of conduct laid down for it by international law.[1]

How does it happen that international law recognizes the
existence of such an attitude of legal indifference to the justice
or injustice of the war, requiring the neutral to stand on the
side-lines, as it were, and follow a course of conduct that
makes no distinction between the guilty and the innocent? The
answer lies in the strange fact that war itself is a legal procedure, that international law still recognizes the right of the
individual nation to take the law into its own hands and prose-
cute its claims by its own armed force. The efforts made of re-

[1] Of course a nation may take the risk of being "benevolently neutral,"
as many have done; it may even go so far as to be "not neutral but merely
non-belligerent," as certain nations are doing today. But this is a risky business, though maybe no more risky than just being a small "correct" neutral.

cent years to restrict this right are well known to us, and we
shall discuss them in detail later.[2] For the moment it is sufficient to say that war, although condemned and outlawed in
numerous treaties, was able to reassert itself successfully as a
legal procedure when Great Britain formally declared on September 3, 1939, that, in consequence of the hostilities of Germany against Poland, a "state of war" existed between His
Majesty's Government and the Government of Germany.

War being a legal procedure, neutrality becomes the lot of
those who choose to stay out of war. If this should seem to involve acquiescence in the commission of crime the defense
would be, for the United States at any rate, that there is no
accepted procedure for distinguishing between right and wrong
in international relations, and that in the absence of such a
procedure there is no other course but to treat both parties
alike.[3] Neutrality may thus be said to be the result of a disor-
ganized, or rather unorganized world society, a society which
has developed highly elaborate rules of international conduct
in matters of lesser consequence, but which has been unable to
assert its authority to the extent of restraining acts of violence
by the collective power of the whole community.[4] How the status of neutrality is regarded as consistent with international
"law," through what phases it has passed, what practical conditions underlie its inconsistencies, what criticism has been
made of it upon moral grounds, are all questions that bear vitally upon the future of an organized world society.[5]

Neutrality the result of an unorganized world society

[2] See below, p. 25.

[3] The procedure could readily enough be worked out. It is just that we
cannot see our national interest in doing so. See below, pp. 26 ff.

[4] See C. G. Fenwick, *International Law,* Chapter II, Sec. D.

[5] The literature on the subject is voluminous. See, in particular, Clyde
Eagleton, *Analysis of the Problem of War* (1937); Quincy Wright, "The Fu-
ture of Neutrality," *International Conciliation,* No. 242 (1928); *Collective
Security,* International Studies Conference, 1935.

8

*The feudal
system
precludes
neutrality*

In the late Middle Ages, when Europe was still dominated by the feudal system, there was little room for the development of a formal law of neutrality. The justice or injustice of a particular war was, indeed, a matter of great consequence to the Canonists and the Schoolmen.[6] Elaborate rules were drawn up to determine the grounds of a just war. The modern attitude of waiving aside an obligation to distinguish between an aggressor nation and the victim of aggression would have met with strong condemnation. To St. Thomas Aquinas, as to St. Augustine some eight centuries earlier, the principle at issue was quite clear : rulers were bound by the same moral obligations that were binding upon their individual subjects.[7] There might be difficulty in determining whether in certain complicated circumstances a particular ruler was or was not justified in resorting to war; but there could be no doubt that his conduct was amenable to the moral law. The difficulty lay not in the absence of standards of moral conduct which kings and princes were bound to observe, but in the absence of a central authority strong enough to enforce compliance with those standards. Moreover, by the very principles of the feudal system the successive strata of underlords and feudal tenants were obligated by the conditions of their tenure to be loyal to their overlords, so that they were in no position to exercise an

[6] See Alfred Vanderpol, *La doctrine scolastique du droit de guerre* (Paris, 1919) ; Robert Regout, *La doctrine de la guerre juste de Saint Augustin à nos jours* (Paris, 1935) ; James Brown Scott, *The Spanish Origin of International Law*, Part I (Oxford: Clarendon Press, 1934-) ; Joachim von Elbe, "The Evolution of the Concept of the Just War in International Law," *American Journal of International Law*, XXXIII (1939), 665.

[7] A recent reiteration of the traditional doctrine may be found in the first encyclical of Pope Pius XII. Text in *The New York Times*, October 28, 1939, pp. 8-9. See, also, the Pope's Allocution, *In Questo Giorno*, on Christmas Eve, 1939, and his reply, on January 7, 1940, to President Roosevelt's letter of December 23, 1939. (Department of State *Bulletin*, December 23, February 3).

independent moral judgment and pass upon his conduct. Under such circumstances, while a particular prince might succeed in avoiding participation in one of the numerous dynastic quarrels of the time, it was his statesmanship that secured him immunity, not any right he might have to be neutral.

With the loosening of the bonds of the Holy Roman Empire *Grotius* and the formation of independent national states a period that *and the* was little short of anarchy ensued in which each nation's hand *duty of* was against its neighbor and no state was certain of its rights *moral* or its obligations. The principle of unity that had dominated *judgment* the Empire was being replaced by the principle of the balance of power, which was at first equally hostile to the conception of neutral states. It is significant that the great theologians, Vitoria and Suárez, who sought to restrain the new "sovereign" rulers by appeals to the fundamental rules of moral conduct and who both kept alive the conception of a society of nations,[8] found no place in their writings for a discussion of the status of neutrality. It was not until the great treatise of Grotius on the *Law of War and of Peace,* published in 1625, that we find a foreshadowing of the neutrality that was to be. But the influence of the moral law, which had dominated the thought of the Canonists, was still strong with Grotius. Hence, while he recognizes the fact that a nation might remain neutral, he also recognizes that moral considerations might lead a nation to take sides in a war. He speaks of neutrals as "those who in time of war are in a position between the contending parties"— *(De his qui in bello medii sunt).* He expects them to look into the merits of the controversy and to take sides accordingly.[9]

[8] See John Eppstein, *The Catholic Tradition of the Law of Nations* (London: Carnegie Endowment for International Peace, 1935).

[9] The expression, "Back to Grotius," heard so frequently among scholars in the post-World War period, meant back to the principle of distinguishing between right and wrong in the conduct of nations, away from the later doctrine of Vattel and his successors that one nation may not sit in judgment upon another.

Here the great writer seems to have been more moral than practical. For with the authority of the Holy Roman Empire practically at an end, if an individual state took sides it did so at its own risk.

The in-
fluence of
commerce

During the century succeeding Grotius, as during the century preceding him, the commercial interests of the leading maritime states exercised an important influence upon the development of neutrality. Neutral states whose vessels were engaged in the carrying trade sought by treaty and otherwise to protect their commerce against the effects of war. The Consolato del Mare of the fifteenth century had made the ownership of goods the test of liability to capture. Holland, formally recognized as sovereign and independent by the Peace of Westphalia, began in 1650 to conclude treaties stipulating that "free ships," that is, neutral ships, should make "free goods." The rules of contraband laid down by Grotius, himself a Dutchman who had in his earlier years championed the freedom of the seas, were elaborated and rendered more precise. Perhaps it might be said that the growing importance of international trade, combined with the naval power of the neutral states engaged in it, was as much responsible as any other single factor for the new conception of the "rights" of a neutral.[10]

The con-
tribution
of Vattel

The publication in the year 1758 of a treatise on the Law of Nations by the Swiss diplomat and publicist, Vattel, marks a significant advance in the recognition of neutrality as a status carrying with it definite rights and duties. Unfortunately, Vattel built up his system of international law upon the philosophical basis of a "law of nature" quite different from that of the Schoolmen. It was all very well for Vattel to argue that

[10] For details, see the valuable work of Philip C. Jessup and Francis Deák, *Neutrality, Its History, Economics and Law* (Columbia University Press, 1935-1936), Vol. I.

states were corporate persons whose common will was but the outcome of the united wills of their citizens, so that they were bound by the same laws of nature by which individual citizens were bound. But when he argued that nations were still living in a "state of nature," and that in consequence of the absence of a supreme authority capable of deciding between them there were cases in which each nation must be allowed its own interpretation of the law of nature, that is to say, must be permitted to be the judge in its own case, he gave an argument to sovereign states which they put to good use.

For the rest, Vattel's description of the rights and duties of neutrality, while not on all points in accord with later law, sets forth an advanced standard of neutral conduct which was to influence greatly the policies of American statesmen and writers. Being published shortly before the Revolution and being, in spite of serious defects, liberal in its outlook, Vattel's treatise became the authoritative textbook of the State Department and of the Federal courts. If his method was deductive and based in part upon false principles, his practical judgments were on the whole sound; and his Swiss origin made him particularly sensitive to rights and obligations conditioning the status of the neutral state.[11]

The American Republic was but four years old when war broke out between Great Britain and France in 1793. Once more the two powerful combatants sought each to bring the other to terms by cutting off its supplies from overseas and destroying its commerce with the rest of the world. Could the United States remain aloof from the conflict? There was the

THE STRUGGLE FOR NEU- TRALITY: *The Act of 1794*

[11] See the Introduction, by De Lapradelle, to the translation of Vattel's treatise published by the Carnegie Institution of Washington, 1916; also, C. G. Fenwick, "The Authority of Vattel," *American Polictical Science Review,* VII, 395; VIII, 375; James L. Brierly, *Law of Nations,* (2d ed., Oxford; Clarendon Press, 1936) pp. 29 ff.

treaty of 1778 with France which had been entered into during the dark hours of the Revolution, calling for the defense of the French possessions in America and for a "benevolent neutrality" in other respects. Fortunately no issue was raised by France on the first point; and Washington, believing that the privileges promised to French ships in the ports of the United States need not be incompatible with the position of neutrality, issued a formal proclamation of neutrality on April 22, 1793. France, however, while not contesting the position of formal neutrality taken by Washington, sought to extend the privileges granted by the treaty, and the enthusiasm of Citizen Genêt led him to believe that he could bring popular pressure to force the hand of the government. Secretary of State Jefferson, however, in spite of his French sympathies, refused to yield on essential points, such as the arming of ships in American ports; and it was soon seen that, if the neutral position assumed by the United States was to be maintained in fact, it would be necessary to pass legislation restraining the acts of individual citizens who might be tempted, whether from love for the Revolutionary cause or for material gain, to compromise the position taken by the government. The result was the passage of the Neutrality Act of 1794, which, as we shall see, was an important factor in the development of a more consistent standard of neutral duty than had yet prevailed.[12]

Neutrality leads to "isolation" The recall of Citizen Genêt in consequence of his overzealous efforts to secure an interpretation of the treaty of 1778 helpful to the French cause did not put an end to the efforts of the French government to influence the conduct of the United States in its favor. Perhaps the least tactful measure that could have been taken was the open intervention of the

[12] See C. G. Fenwick, *The Neutrality Laws of the United States* (1912), pp. 15-32; Charles S. Hyneman, *The First American Neutrality* (University of Illinois Press, 1934).

French agents against the reelection of President Washington in 1796. It was this intermeddling in the domestic politics of the country that led to the strong statement by Washington on September 3, 1796, which has since become a cardinal principle of the foreign policy of the United States and has been interpreted to justify a policy of isolation far broader than the strict neutrality contemplated in the Farewell Address. Washington was the most practical of statesmen, the least given to dogmatic generalizations; and yet the reverence for his name has been used to condemn proposals of international cooperation for the prevention of war which have not the remotest resemblance to the "combinations and collisions" denounced by him on that memorable occasion.

But the failure of the French intrigues during Washington's *Neutrality* administration merely marked the beginning of the struggle of *breaks* the United States to maintain its neutrality. As the war con- *down* tinued and the belligerents became more desperate, each side was led to impose additional restrictions upon neutral trade. What they could not justify on the ground of normal belligerent rights they undertook to justify each on the ground of retaliation for the excesses of the other. What followed is a familiar story. We were almost at war with France in 1798; we tried putting embargoes upon the shipping of the belligerents; we tried passing acts to restrain our citizens from trade to which they were legally entitled but in which we could not effectively protect them, and we lifted the restrictions when they complained too loudly; we tried bargaining with the belligerents; and finally we were drawn into the war.[13] The struggle to remain neutral was lost. It was lost, as we shall see later, be-

[13] The story of the successive embargo and non-intercourse acts may be found in John H. Latané *A History of American Foreign Policy* (1st. ed., 1927), Chapter VI, "The Struggle for Neutral Rights"; Samuel F. Bemis, *A Diplomatic History of the United States* (1936), Chapter IX.

cause we were not willing to pay the price of remaining neutral on the belligerents' terms.[14]

By the close of the nineteenth century, the growth in power of the United States and the generations of peace among Great Britain, France, and Spain had changed the position of neutrals from one of sufferance by to one of equality with the belligerents. Neutrality had become "respectable." It was accepted that in future wars the neutrals would be able to hold their own against undue claims by the belligerents, that they might be able by their power and prestige to maintain their position without being drawn into war to defend it. But the specter of war, which it seemed had been laid for a while, had not been exorcised. The rivalry in armaments was a constant threat to the peace; and the growing economic competition among the leading industrial powers contained the probable motives of future conflict. Faced with this situation the powers met at the Hague Peace Conference of 1899. There, after establishing the inadequate Hague Court of Arbitration, they undertook to draw up a code of the laws of war, and with it a Convention Respecting the Rights and Duties of Neutral Powers and Persons in Case of War on Land. Again at the second Hague Peace Conference of 1907 the codification of the laws of war took precedence of a constructive program of peace. This time a long diplomatic struggle took place among the powers that thought of themselves as probable belligerents in the next war and those that expected to be neutral; a struggle which was complicated within the group of probable belligerents by questions of naval power, size of merchant marine, colonial possessions, and other factors bearing upon the success of warfare at sea.[15]

[14] See below, Chapter V.

[15] A good account of the conflicting forces may be found in A. Pearce Higgins, *The Hague Peace Conferences and Other International Conferences Concerning the Laws and Usages of War* (Cambridge University Press, 1909), pp. 290, 457.

If the Hague Convention Concerning the Rights and Duties of
Neutral Powers in Naval War settled a number of questions in
favor of neutrals, it left an equal number unsettled, notably
the issue of blockade and contraband upon which the degree
of belligerent interference with neutral trade depended. These
the London Naval Conference of 1908-1909 attempted to set-
tle;[16] but the compromise Declaration of London there adopted
had not yet been ratified when the World War broke out. The
diplomatic struggle between neutrals and belligerents at the
Hague and the London Conferences now found itself engaged
with concrete issues instead of academic problems.

The World War had not been in progress for more than a NEUTRAL-
few months before it was realized that the elaborate rules of ITY CHAL-
neutrality drawn up by the Hague Conferences and the Lon- LENGED,
don Naval Conference had far from solved the conflicts of 1914-1917
interest between belligerents and neutrals. In the first place,
since the Declaration of London had not yet been ratified by
the leading powers whose activities it was intended to regulate, the important issues of blockade and contraband were left
to the decision of the older customary law whose uncertainties
the Declaration had sought to correct. Secondly, while the
Hague Conventions prescribing the rights and duties of neutrals had been ratified by the leading powers, they had not been
ratified by Serbia, with the result that they were not technically binding on the other belligerents, although they continued to form a standard that might be appealed to as repre-
senting on the whole a consensus of opinion as to established
practice. It was soon seen, however, that new instrumentalities
and new methods of warfare were to make many of the older
rules obsolete, or at any rate were to be offered as excuses by

[16] The General Report on the Declaration of London, showing the com-
promises made between the conflicting interests may be found in A. Pearce
Higgins, *op. cit.*, p. 567.

16   the belligerents for setting aside the traditional law. Particularly was this true of the invention of the submarine, the effective use of which against merchant shipping made impossible the observance of the customary rules with respect to the safety of passengers and crew.[17]

President   After two years of controversy between the United States
Wilson's   and both belligerents President Wilson became convinced that
answer   neutrality itself was an inherently untenable position, which must inevitably lead to sharp controversies with the belligerents. The only possible solution for the conflicts of vital national interests to which neutrality gave rise was to abolish altogether the war system which occasioned them. "The business of neutrality is over," he said in his address to the Senate on October 26, 1916. No nation must henceforth be permitted to declare war and set in motion forces so destructive to the normal commerce of peaceful nations; the whole international community must combine to put an end to lawlessness. The entrance of the United States into the war on April 6, 1917, was thus not merely in defense of its technical neutral rights, but in defense of the right of all nations to be free from the disruptive effects of war even if they could succeed in remaining neutral. In that sense the war became on the part of the United States a "war to end war," in spite of the irony that has since attended the use of that phrase.[18] Moreover, in as much as President Wilson was convinced that it was not the German people but their military leaders who were responsible for the war, the participation in the war by the United States had as its object "to make the world safe for democracy." Here the

[17] The issues involved in the many controversies will be discussed under separate headings in later chapters.

[18] See above, p. 1. The foreign policy of President Wilson is sympathetically treated in Charles Seymour, *American Neutrality, 1914-1917* (Yale University Press, 1935).

President's position was somewhat academic, inasmuch as the record of the democracies, whichever nations might be included within that group, was not above reproach.

17

NEUTRAL-
ITY QUI-
ESCENT
*Effect
of the
League
Covenant*

The Covenant of the League of Nations put an end in principle to the status of neutrality. The obligations of mutual defense created by Article 10 made it necessary for every member of the League to take part in the common defense of the victim of an act of aggression. Moreover, Article 11, by making any war or threat of war "a matter of concern" to all members of the League whether they were directly involved in it or not, directly repudiated the principle of neutrality; while Article 16, by making a war begun in violation of the Covenant a war against all of the members of the League, automatically fixed the legal position of the members of the League whether they subsequently resorted to sanctions or not.[19] The failure of the United States to accept the obligations of the Covenant of the League of Nations created a situation in which it was difficult to reconcile treaty obligations with traditional customary law. Technically the Covenant was no more than a multilateral treaty, creating obligations for the parties to it, but leaving the status of nonsignatory states just what it was before the treaty. Yet inasmuch as the Covenant, by the accession of new signatories, soon included all of the former great powers except Germany, Russia, and the United States, and practically all of the other powers, it was difficult for the international lawyer to determine how much was left of the old common law of neutrality in the presence of the new "legislation," if that term can be used, repudiating it.[20]

[19] The literature on the subject is voluminous. See, in particular, Felix Morley, *The Society of Nations*, (Washington: The Brookings Institution, 1932); Alfred Eckhard Zimmern, *The League of Nations and the Rule of Law, 1918-1935* (London: The Macmillan Company, 1936).

[20] See below, pp. 29 ff.

For some ten years the problem remained little more than an academic one, of much interest to scholars but of little concern to the public at large. So long as the authority of the League appeared equal to the task of maintaining the peace, or so long at any rate as its authority was not successfully challenged, it was a matter of no practical consequence what attitude the United States would take in the event the League should find itself at war with an aggressor and the United States would have to decide whether it should acquiesce in the sanctions taken by the League or should assert its traditional rights as a neutral. The conclusion of the Locarno treaties, which seemed to be a reinsurance of peace in the storm-center of Europe, strengthened the prestige of the League; while the admission of Germany into the League in 1926 appeared for the time to have removed the most serious obstacle to the unanimity necessary to effective action. All those in the United States who had favored the entrance of the United States into the League in order to strengthen the League's authority and to make the system of collective security more truly collective were encouraged to hope that the League might now be able to carry out its objects even without the aid of the United States. The League seemed to have passed the danger point, and the ultimate cooperation of the United States could come in its own due time. With the prospects against another war, there was no need of coming to definite conclusions on the question whether the United States could make legal claims under a law of neutrality that seemed to have lost its meaning.

Codifica-
tion of
laws
of war
In the meantime the technical survival of the old law of neutrality, in spite of the obligations assumed by the members of the League of Nations, was suggested in the several efforts that were made to codify certain branches of the law of war. In 1922, at the close of the Washington Conference, a commission of jurists was appointed to consider the question whether

the existing rules of international law adequately covered new
methods of attack and defense resulting from the new agencies
of warfare developed since 1907. Two sets of rules were prepared, the first dealing with the control of radio in time of war
and the second dealing with aerial warfare. Both sets dealt
with war and neutrality without reference to the provisions of
the League Covenant.[21] No action, however, was taken upon
them, and little notice seems to have been taken of their assumption that in the possible war which they contemplated the
status of neutrals would follow the traditional lines.

The introduction in February, 1928, by Senator Borah of a
resolution calling for a restatement of the rules of maritime
law as preliminary material for the coming conference on the
Limitation of Naval Armaments raised the issue of neutrality
in more concrete form. Inasmuch as the contemplated plans
for disarmament were to be worked out without reference to
the system of collective security provided for in the Covenant
of the League of Nations it seemed necessary that there should
be some agreement upon the rules governing the conduct of
belligerents and neutrals. The size of the navy of the United
States would naturally be contingent upon the nature of the
interests it was to protect, and prominent among those interests
were the rights of neutral trade. As against this position the
advocates of cooperation with the League argued that it was
impossible to codify the old law of neutrality, because that had
been set aside by obligations assumed by the members of the
League under the Covenant; and that unless the United States
was prepared to accept some modification of the old law by
way of recognition of possible common action by the League

[21] For the texts of the draft codes, see *Am. Journal of Int. Law*, XVII
(1923), Supp., 242, 245. For comment see John Bassett Moore, *International
Law and Some Current Illusions* (1924), pp. 210 ff.

*The
Havana
Conven-
tion on
Maritime
Neutrality*

against an aggressor there was no basis for an agreement.[22] The resolution was not pressed to a vote.

At the Sixth International Conference of American States held at Havana, in 1928, the assembled delegates undertook to codify the laws of maritime neutrality. The basis of the codification was the Hague Convention of 1907 concerning the Rights and Duties of Neutral Powers in Naval War, which, although not ratified by many of the Latin American states, had actually been adopted by most of them as their rule of conduct during the World War. It is difficult to find justification for the convention, inasmuch as non-American maritime states would obviously not be bound by any new rules. Possibly there was an assumption, later to be formulated in more precise terms, that greater authority might attach to the rules adopted if the American states all took the same position on controversial points. The issue of the old law of neutrality versus the obligations created by the Covenant of the League of Nations was evaded. Article 28 of the convention merely declared that "the present convention does not affect obligations previously undertaken by the contracting parties through international agreements.[23]

NEUTRAL-
ITY RE-
VIVED:
THE
CHACO
WAR

When Paraguay formally declared war upon Bolivia in 1933, the neighbouring countries promptly declared their neutrality; Argentina, Chile, and Peru announcing that their conduct as neutrals would be governed by the rules set forth in the Hague Conventions of 1907, while Peru and Chile added that the rules of the Declaration of London would also apply. Brazil formulated regulations of its own, which conformed in general

[22] This argument was effectively presented by Manley O. Hudson in *The New York Times,* Sec. 3, pp. 1, 6, March 11, 1928.

[23] For the text of the convention, see *Am. Journal of Int. Law,* XXII (1928), Supp., 124; for comment, see James W. Garner, "The Pan American Convention on Maritime Neutrality," *ibid.,* XXVI (1932), 574.

to those of the Hague Convention and the Declaration of London. Since the Council of the League of Nations did not call for discriminatory sanctions or for measures which were not within the rights and duties of neutrals under the traditional law, no conclusions can be drawn as to the relative legal value attributed by the three states that were members of the League to the two sets of obligations under the particular circumstances.[24]

It is doubtless in the light of the conditions arising from the war between Bolivia and Paraguay that we must read the somewhat cryptic provisions in the Anti-War Treaty of Non-Aggression and Conciliation, the Saavedra Lamas Pact, of October 10, 1933.[25] Article 3 of the treaty provides that, in case of noncompliance with the obligations of nonaggression and pacific settlement contained in the preceding articles, the contracting states were to "adopt in their character as neutrals a common and solidary attitude," and were to "exercise the political, juridical, or economic means authorized by international law." The final clause of the same article carried the proviso that this was "subject to the attitude that may be incumbent on them by virtue of other collective treaties (clearly including, if not confined to the Covenant of the League of Nations) to which such states are signatories." The problem was left unsettled how a "common and solidary attitude" was to be maintained if the American states that were members of the League of Nations were called upon to discriminate against an

[24] On the legal issues arising in connection with the war in the Chaco, see C. G. Fenwick, "The Arms Embargo against Bolivia and Paraguay," *Am. Journal of Int. Law*, XXVIII (1934), 534; L. H. Woolsey, "The Chaco Dispute," *ibid.*, 724.

[25] For the text of the treaty, see *Am. Journal of Int. Law*, XXVIII (1934), Supp., 79; *United States Treaty Series*, No. 906.

aggressor while the United States stood by the traditional law.[26]

At the Inter-American Conference for the Maintenance of Peace, held at Buenos Aires in 1936, the same purpose of maintaining a "common and solidary" neutral attitude is affirmed in the terms of Article 6 of the Convention to Coordinate, Extend, and Assure the Fulfillment of the Existing Treaties between the American States.[27] Even greater logical inconsistencies, however, appear in the provision that this shall be "without prejudice to the universal principles of neutrality provided for in the case of an international war outside of America and without affecting the duties contracted by those American States members of the League of Nations," as if it were possible under any circumstances to meet both of those situations at once. The second paragraph of Article 6 goes on to provide that the contracting parties might consider "the imposition of prohibitions or restrictions on the sale or shipment of arms, munitions and implements of war, loans or other financial help to the States in conflict . . . without detriment to their obligations derived from other treaties to which they are or may become parties." Here was more specific ground of conflict between the old law of neutrality and possible new obligations of discrimination. Notwithstanding the protective provisos of the above article, a separate article (7) was introduced to the effect that nothing in the convention should be understood as affecting the rights and duties of the parties which were at the same time members of the League of Nations. Colombia felt it necessary to enter an express reser-

[26] While the original signatories of the treaty were the American states, it was provided (Article 16) that the treaty should remain open to the adherence of all states. That only made the problem of a common and solidary neutral attitude the more insoluble.

[27] For the text of the treaty see *Am. Journal of Int. Law*, XXXI (1937), Supp., 53 ff.; Pan American Union, *Congress and Conference Series*, No. 22, p. 37.

vation interpreting the phrase "in their character as neutrals" as implying "a new concept of international law which allows a distinction to be drawn between the aggressor and the attacked, and to treat them differently"; and the Colombian delegation proceeded to define the acts which should be held to fix the character of an "aggressor." Obviously the United States did not understand the provisions of Articles 5 and 6 in the sense given to them by Colombia. But any further attempts at explanation would only have emphasized the confusion created by the two legally irreconciliable positions.[28]

Small European states announce neutrality

While the Latin American states were trying to adjust their obligations under the Covenant of the League of Nations with the desire of the United States to develop a common policy of neutrality for the western hemisphere, the clouds of war were gathering in Europe. The failure of the League to check the invasion of Manchuria by Japan in 1931-1933 had shaken the faith of many of the smaller nations of Europe in the system of collective security. Their faith was still further shaken by the inability of the League to restrain Italy in its conquest of Abyssinia. It was one thing for them to cooperate in sanctions against Italy so long as the preponderance of the powers enforcing the sanctions might overawe Italy and prevent forcible resistance. But if the authority of the League was to be openly resisted by Italy and war, possibly a general European war, was to result, then it might be safer for them to fall back upon the old law of neutrality under which some of them had found safety during the World War. In consequence, in the years succeeding 1936, one by one, Norway, Sweden, Denmark, Holland, Belgium, Switzerland, and others announced that in the event of war it was their intention to maintain their neu-

[28] For comment on other aspects of the treaty, see C. G. Fenwick, "The Inter-American Conference for the Maintenance of Peace," *Am. Journal of Int. Law*, XXXI (1937), 201.

trality under the traditional law. This attitude was all the more confirmed by the settlement of the Sudeten controversy by Great Britain, France, and Germany at Munich in September, 1938, without reference to the Council or the Assembly of the League. War was clearly on the horizon, and for the smaller nations the best hope of escaping it seemed to lie in the neutrality of 1914.

With the declaration of war by Great Britain against Germany on September 3, 1939, formal declarations of neutrality came from all but a few of the states not directly participants in it. The Proclamation of Neutrality of the United States, issued on September 5, followed the traditional lines of proclamations in past wars, reciting the existence of a "state of war," that the United States was on terms of friendship and amity with the contending powers and that, in consequence, certain provisions of the Penal Code of 1909, intended to protect the neutrality of the United States, were applicable.[29] It was assumed by the United States without question that the legal relations between neutrals and belligerents would be conducted on the basis of the rights and duties of the traditional law of neutrality. Thus the neutrals were back once more to the law of 1914, to begin again the controversies with belligerents that had marked the long course of the World War.

[29] These provisions of the Penal Code, providing for the enforcement of the neutral duties of the United States under the traditional rules of international law (see below, p. 116) must be sharply distinguished from the "neutrality" provisions of the Joint Resolution of 1937 (see below, p. 44) which were put into effect the same day. For the text of the Neutrality Proclamation, see Appendix A.

III. RECENT NEUTRALITY LEGISLATION
OF THE UNITED STATES

On November 11, 1921, three years after the Armistice, the
United States signed a separate treaty of peace with Germany. With that treaty all question of the ratification of the
Treaty of Versailles, and with it the Covenant of the League
of Nations, came to an end. But the advocates of the entrance
of the United States into the League, believing that the hope
of a permanent peace lay in the system of collective security
established by the League, were naturally not to be deterred
by the temporary defeat of their cause. For some years their
efforts were chiefly confined to the advocacy of the cooperation of the United States with the social and economic activities of the League, leaving political cooperation to come in its
own due time. The question of membership of the United
States in the Permanent Court of International Justice preoc-
cupied their efforts for a time in 1926. Then, on August 27,
1928, came the conclusion of the Kellogg Pact to test whether
the cooperation of the United States in the prevention of war
was to be more than a perfunctory gesture. What would the
United States *do* by way of restraining aggression? What concrete action would it take to prevent war rather than seek to
avoid the consequences of war? Was the policy of isolation and
neutrality to stand forever in the way of putting the power of
the United States on the side of law and order?

THE
POST-WAR
PEACE
POLICY
OF THE
UNITED
STATES

The Kellogg Pact seemed in its terms little more than a New Year's resolution.[1] The contracting powers condemned recourse to war for the solution of international controversies; they renounced war as an instrument of national policy; they agreed that the settlement of disputes of whatever kind should never be sought except by pacific means. Beyond that the Pact did not go. It made no provision for measures of enforcement in case of its violation; it set up no machinery even to determine whether there had been a violation. Its broad "outlawry" of war, which in the text of the treaty went even further than the provisions of the Covenant of the League of Nations, was limited and qualified by a covering letter of Secretary Kellogg in which the right of self-defense was reserved in such general terms as to permit escape from the obligations of the Pact even more easily than might be done under Article 15 of the Covenant.[2] But for all that the Kellogg Pact stood as a symbol of the recognition by the United States, late indeed but still vitally important, that it could not remain indifferent to the efforts that were being made in Europe to develop and strengthen the machinery of peace.[3] Clearly the United States, as the advocates of the League of Nations saw it, could not now adopt an attitude of indifference and neutrality if a signatory of the pact were to flaunt its obligations. The fact that the signatories of the pact were also for the most part members of the League

[1] The technical name of the Pact is "Treaty for the Renunciation of War," *U. S. Treaty Series*, No. 796; C. G. Fenwick, *International Law*, Appendix C.

[2] Both the friends of the League of Nations and its opponents were fully aware of the legal weaknesses of the Pact; but for their own reasons both groups avoided putting too much emphasis upon them.

[3] See James T. Shotwell, *War as an Instrument of National Policy* (1929), where the background of the Kellogg Pact may be found and an analysis of its meaning and scope; Denys P. Myers, *Origin and Conclusion of the Paris Pact* (World Peace Foundation, 1929).

of Nations meant to the advocates of the League that the 27
United States would now lend its indirect support to the League
system.

*Efforts to
implement
the Pact*

Among the early efforts made in Congress to "implement"
the Kellogg Pact was the introduction by Senator Capper, in
February, 1929, of a resolution calling for a prohibition of the
export of arms and munitions of war to any country which the
President declared to have violated the pact. Further, it was
declared to be the policy of the United States not to protect
its nationals in case they should give aid and comfort to a nation that had committed a breach of the pact. The resolution
thus supplemented its embargo on arms by indirect pressure
upon individuals who might by trade in other articles, or by
loans or other forms of assistance, give help to a violator of
the pact.[4]

*The doc-
trine of
nonrecog-
nition*

The Capper Resolution was still pending when the invasion
of Manchuria by Japan in the summer of 1931 raised a new
problem of neutrality in relation to a violation of the Nine
Power Treaty. On January 7, 1932, Secretary Stimson issued
a statement declaring that the United States could not "admit
the legality of any situation *de facto*," nor did it "intend to
recognize any situation, treaty or agreement which may be
brought about by means contrary to the covenants and obligations of the Pact of Paris of August 27, 1928."[5] This formal
official statement would doubtless have been incompatible with
neutrality had the hostilities of Japan in Manchuria constituted
a technical state of war. Seven months later, on August 8,
Secretary Stimson expressed the opinion that while "under

[4] A revised form of the Capper Resolution was introduced into the Senate in April, 1932, extending its provisions to war supplies and to commercial transactions, and incorporating the new nonrecognition doctrine. See
B. H. Williams, *American Diplomacy, Policies and Practice* (1936), p. 335.

[5] See in this connection, Quincy Wright, "The Stimson Note of January
7, 1932," *Am. Journal of Int. Law.*, XXVI (1932), 342.

the former concepts of international law" states not parties to
a conflict could only exercise "a strict neutrality alike towards
the injured and the aggressor," . . . "now under the covenants
of the Briand-Kellogg Pact such a conflict becomes of concern
to everybody connected with the pact." The obligations of the
pact thus carried the implication that in the event of its violation the United States would consult with the other signatories
and modify its normal policy of impartiality according to the
decision taken.[6]

The offer   The suggestion of "consultation" by the United States with
of con-   other signatories of the Kellogg Pact in the event that a par-
sultation   ticular state should repudiate its obligations was carried still
further in 1933 by Norman Davis, delegate of the United
States at the Geneva Conference on the Limitation of Armaments. On the understanding that the limitation of armaments
contemplated by the conference could be secured, Mr. Davis
made the following important statement: "We are willing to
consult with other states in case of a threat to the peace with
a view to averting a conflict. Further than that, in the event
that the states in conference determine that a state has been
guilty of a breach of peace in violation of its international obligations and take measures against a violator, if we concur in
the judgement rendered as to the responsible and guilty party,
we will refrain from any action tending to defeat such collec-

[6] See C. G. Fenwick, "The Implication of Consultation in the Pact of
Paris," *Am. Journal of Int. Law,* XXVI (1932), 789; Quincy Wright, "The
Meaning of the Pact of Paris," *ibid.,* XXVII (1933), 57; Quincy Wright
and Clyde Eagleton, "Neutrality and Neutral Rights Following the Pact of
Paris for the Renunciation of War," *Proceedings, American Society of In-
ternational Law,* 1930, pp. 79, 87.

So general was the desire among all elements of public opinion to develop
the Kellogg Pact into an instrument of closer cooperation with other nations
for the maintenance of peace that both the Republican and the Democratic
party platforms of 1932 approved the idea of "consultation" with other
nations as a means of maintaining the authority of the Pact.

tive effort which the states may thus make to restore peace."
This conditional offer of cooperation, although in negative form, marks perhaps the high-water mark of the willingness of the United States Government to cooperate with the League in the maintenance of peace.[7]

The debate on neutrality which now began with renewed intensity was destined to last until finally the outbreak of war in 1939 marked the defeat of those who had hoped that war might be prevented if the weight of the United States could be thrown into the balance against aggression.[8] The guiding principle of those who urged the cooperation of the United States in the collective security system of the League was that, if the

Neutrality pro and con

[7] On the subject of consultation as a means for the maintenance of peace see Russell M. Cooper, *American Consultation in World Affairs for the Preservation of Peace* (1934); Philip C. Jessup, *International Security*, p. 64 ff., (Council on Foreign Relations, 1935); John Bassett Moore, "An Appeal to Reason," *Foreign Affairs*, July, 1933, condemns the suggested commitment of the United States to a "consultative pact," as do Edwin M. Borchard and William P. Lage, *Neutrality for the United States* (Yale University Press, 1937), pp. 299 ff.

[8] The literature on the subject is extensive. See, in particular, *Proceedings, American Society of International Law*, 1930, pp. 79 ff., and *ibid.*, 1933, pp. 55 ff., where both sides are presented; Quincy Wright, "The Future of Neutrality," *International Conciliation*, No. 242 (1928); Clyde Eagleton, "The Attempt to Define Aggression," *ibid.*, No. 264 (1930); Philip C. Jessup, *International Security* (Council on Foreign Relations, 1935); Philip C. Jessup and Francis Deák, *Neutrality, Its History, Economics and Law*, Vol. IV. The Harvard Draft Convention on Rights and Duties of States in Case of Aggression, *Am. Journal of Int. Law*, XXXIII (1939), No. 4, Sec. 2, constitutes a most valuable analysis of the whole problem distinguishing between "aggressors," "defending states," "co-defending states," and "supporting states," as the several categories are designated. The reporter was Professor Philip C. Jessup. The draft is preceded by an elaborate bibliography on aggression by Professor Clyde Eagleton. See also, Herbert W. Briggs and Raymond Leslie Buell, "American Neutrality in a Future War," *Foreign Policy Reports*, April 10, 1935, where the opposing points of view are carefully examined.

30   United States would not become an active partner in the
League, it should at least adjust its policies so as not to defeat
the efforts of the League to restrain acts of aggression. Neutrality in the traditional sense of treating both sides alike
meant in practice making no distinction between right and
wrong. Neutrality was the negation of law and order; it was
the product of international anarchy; it was contrary to the
fundamental conceptions of law and order which had prevailed
between the citizens of every civilized state; it would not do
for the United States to hold out alone against the great body
of the nations in their effort to establish new legal principles
as the basis of a more secure peace.

Neutral   What this meant in practice was that the United States, if it
rights   would not openly cooperate in the collective security system,
and col-   should recognize at least that the great body of the nations,
lective   including at that time all but Russia and Turkey, were seeking
security   to make that system work, and should therefore abandon policies of neutrality which belonged to the old anarchy before the
World War and cooperate with the League to the extent of not
insisting upon the traditional rights of neutral trade when such
trade would prevent the League from enforcing the provisions
of Article 16 of the Covenant. What name should be applied to
such a policy was a matter of no consequence. The "cooperationists," if they may so be described, did not regard police
action by the League as "war" in the traditional sense; hence
they preferred to rule out the whole conception of neutrality
as belonging to a past era in which war had a recognized legal
status.

Peace   In their attack upon the principle of neutrality on the ground
and   of its indifference to the moral issue of right and wrong in the
justice   case of a war of aggression, the cooperationists were not un-
aware of the fact that the policies of the League of Nations

fell far short of the conditions necessary for permanent peace. Peace, it was held, must be based upon two distinct principles: the repression of violence and the promotion of justice. Each was indispensable to the success of the other. But of the two the repression of violence was primary, inasmuch as the resort to violence destroyed the conditions under which the more complicated problem of justice could be effectively considered. If the *status quo* contained elements of injustice, the effort to overthrow it by violence must inevitably result in greater injustice. On the other hand it was clear that if justice was too long delayed, or rather if there seemed to be no hope of obtaining justice by peaceful methods, nations that were in distress would be tempted to take the law into their own hands. The problem, therefore, was to prevent the resort to violence while urging in every way the removal of the conditions that made for violence. In both respects the cooperation of the United States was believed to be not only morally proper, but under certain circumstances essential.

The opposition to the abandonment of neutrality came on the whole from those who had no faith in the League of Nations or any other form of concerted action for the maintenance of peace. There were the time-honored methods of peaceful settlement, conciliation and arbitration. If these procedures would not suffice, methods of coercion certainly would not. Sanctions were nothing more than war in another form; and in the case of the League of Nations, it was held, sanctions were merely the means by which the dominant powers in the League were able to use the League machinery to maintain the iniquitous *status quo* imposed on the vanquished by the Treaty of Versailles. With great irony and scorn the "isolationists," if a name may be pinned to them for convenience, attacked not merely the League but the principle itself of "collective secu-

Isolation and neutrality

rity." [9] It was a principle not of security, but of insecurity; it had no other purpose but to perpetuate the wrongs of Versailles. Let the United States keep out of the whole business. We had tried one war to end war. Was not that lesson enough? Let us take our stand on true and tried neutrality. Washington had said the final word on the subject in his Farewell Address. Nothing had happened to make his advice any the less applicable as the years had gone by.

Divided counsels

Obviously it is only in the most general way that one can attempt to classify the two groups as "cooperationists" and "isolationists." Within each group were those who dissented from the ways and means advocated by others of the same group. Possibly the most significant division in the ranks of the cooperationists was between those who believed in the use of sanctions to restrain acts of aggression and those who were opposed to any form of direct or indirect coercion. Among the isolationists there were those who took their stand upon the old law of neutrality, as it stood in 1914, and those who were prepared to go further and abandon so-called neutral rights if they could thereby isolate the country more completely. Unhappily, political party lines dating from 1920 tended still further to confuse issues complicated enough in themselves. [10]

The Borah Resolution

In the meantime the question of an embargo on shipments of arms came again to the front. During the last months of the Hoover administration Senator Borah, then chairman of the Foreign Relations Committee, introduced a resolution providing that whenever the President should find that the shipment

[9] The volume by Edwin M. Borchard and William P. Lage, *Neutrality for the United States,* is doubtless one of the most effective in its destructive criticism. But see also John Bassett Moore, "An Appeal to Reason," *Foreign Affairs,* July, 1933.

[10] This aspect of the issue may be studied in Denna F. Fleming, *The United States and World Organization, 1920-1933* (Columbia University Press, 1938).

of arms from the United States might promote recourse to
force in a dispute between nations and, "after securing the cooperation of such governments" as he deemed necessary, he
made proclamation of the fact, it should be unlawful to export
arms or munitions of war "to such country or countries as he
may designate." [11] The terms of the resolution, although directed primarily towards the war in the Chaco, were broad
enough to have permitted discriminatory action against Japan,
still carrying on its hostilities in Manchuria in spite of the re-
proofs of Secretary Stimson and of the Assembly of the League
of Nations.[12] A year later, in February, 1934, an amendment,
proposed by Senator Johnson, was adopted by the Committee
requiring that any prohibition of exports under the resolution
should "apply impartially to all the parties to the dispute."
With this amendment the resolution would have been directed
not only against the aggressor but against the victim of aggression; and in consequence the Administration did not press for
its passage.

The war between Bolivia and Paraguay in the Chaco brought   THE
forth a new resolution in May, 1934, giving the President au-   CHACO
thority to apply an arms embargo against both belligerents if   EMBARGO
he found that it would contribute to the reestablishment of   RESOLU-
peace between the two countries. The absence of any provision   TION
for discriminatory action against one or other of the parties on
the basis of violation of treaty obligations kept the resolution
strictly in line with the precedents of 1912 and 1922 and made
possible its passage without delay.[13]

[11] For the text, see Senate Joint Resolution 229, 72d Congress, 2d Session.
[12] See above, p. 27.
[13] For the text, see House Joint Resolution 347, 48 *Statutes at Large*, 811
(May 28, 1934); Francis Deák and Philip C. Jessup, eds., *A Collection of
Neutrality Laws, Regulations and Treaties of Various Countries* (Washington: Carnegie Endowment for International Peace, 1939), II, 1143. The

Up to this time the debate between the advocates and the opponents of cooperation with the League of Nations had been concerned primarily with the effect of an embargo on arms upon a possible resort by the League to sanctions against an aggressor. Advocates of cooperation with the League, while urging a discriminatory embargo because of its value as a deterrent against aggression, accepted somewhat reluctantly an embargo directed against both parties alike, on the ground that at least it would prevent the defeat of sanctions by the League to the extent of denying arms to an aggressor, while the League could assist the victim. Now, with the growing threats of war in Europe, a new group came to the front whose interest in an embargo on shipments of arms centered on the need of protecting the United States against involvement in war not so much by reason of efforts to restrain an aggressor as by reason of the lure of profits from the industries associated with war. This group drew its inspiration from the investigations of the Senate Committee headed by Senator Nye, whose "exposures" of the part played by the munitions industry and the banking interests in the propaganda which influenced the entrance of the United States into the World War had aroused public opinion.[14] A lurid picture was presented of an innocent, and apparently somewhat naïve, people being led unwillingly to war for the sake of protecting the interests of a few captains of

---

proclamation under which the act was brought into effect was revoked November 14, 1935.

The constitutionality of the grant by Congress to the President of discretion as to the specific conditions calling for the application of the embargo resolution was upheld by the Supreme Court in *United States* v. *Curtiss-Wright Export Corporation,* decided December 21, 1936.

[14] A summary of the early hearings before the Nye Committee may be found in William T. Stone, "The Munitions Industry; An Analysis of the Senate Investigation, September 4-21, 1934," *Foreign Policy Reports,* X, No. 20, December 5, 1934.

industry and finance; and a clarion call was formulated: "Take
the profits out of war." [15] The darker the shadow cast by the
impending attack of Italy upon Ethiopia the more urgent
seemed the need of legislation. Congress acted, but put a six
months' limit upon the mandatory provisions of the law.

The Joint Resolution, approved August 31, 1935, provided   *The em-*
that "upon the outbreak or during the progress of war" be-   *bargo*
tween two or more foreign states the President should proclaim *on arms*
the fact and it should thereafter be "unlawful to export arms,
ammunition, or implements of war" from any place in the
United States to any port of the belligerent states or to any
neutral port for transshipment to a belligerent country. A National Munitions Control Board was established to supervise
the registration of persons engaged in the munitions business
and the issuance of licenses for export. Section 3 of the act
made it a separate offense for an American vessel to carry the
forbidden cargoes. So much of the act was "mandatory"; that
is, it left no option to the President but to put the law into
effect once a war broke out. Later sections of the act made it
unlawful for submarines to enter ports of the United States and
for American citizens to travel as passengers on vessels of a
belligerent nation, provided that the President should find that
such restrictions would serve to maintain peace between the
United States and foreign nations, or protect the commercial
interests of the United States and its citizens, or promote the
security of the United States. A broad discretion was thus left
to the President on these points.[16]

[15] See in particular, Gilbert Seldes, *Iron, Blood and Profits; An Exposure
of the World-Wide Munitions Racket* (1934); Helmuth C. Engelbrecht and
F. C. Hanighen, *Merchants of Death; a Study of the International Armament Industry* (1934).

[16] For the text of the act, see Francis Deák and Philip C. Jessup, *op. cit.*,
II, 1100.

Rigid
versus
flexible
legis-
lation

The
Italian-
Ethiopian
War

The debate between the "cooperationists" and the "isolation-ists" now centered upon the issue of mandatory or discretion-ary legislation, or, as it was also described, rigid and flexible legislation. In signing the resolution the President called atten-tion to the need of further consideration of the arms embargo. Neither Congress nor the Executive could "foresee all possible future situations." It was conceivable, he said, that situations might arise in which the "wholly inflexible provisions" of the act might drag us into war instead of keeping us out. While it was the policy of the Government to avoid entanglements, it was also its policy to "cooperate with other similarly minded governments to promote peace." The President thus, in very guarded language, seemed to take the side of those who would have given him discretionary power, in order that the threat of an embargo might operate to deter potential aggressors.

The provisions of the act found prompt application when early in October Italy defied the League of Nations and began open hostilities against Ethiopia. Not only was the mandatory embargo on arms put into effect; but the President promptly proclaimed that American citizens would travel on belligerent vessels at their own risk.[17] Going beyond the terms of the law, the President also warned that trade with the belligerents would be at the risk of the trader, meaning that diplomatic protection would be denied. Here the President was acting purely within his executive powers; and the practical effect of his warning depended upon the actual risk taken by traders, in this case negligible, and their willingness to cooperate volun-tarily with the Administration. This attempt to discourage trade which the law did not prohibit was carried even further by a warning on October 30 against "transactions of any char-acter" with either of the belligerent nations except at the risk

[17] Francis Deák and Philip C. Jessup, *op. cit.*, II, 1227, 1228.

of the trader.[18] Again on November 15 it was announced by the Department of State that the shipment to the belligerents of oil, copper, trucks, scrap iron, and other commodities would be regarded as contrary to the "policy" of the Government and contrary to the "general spirit" of the neutrality act.[19] The President thus indicated clearly his desire, within the limits of the act of 1935 and of his executive powers, not to have the absence of the United States from the counsels of the League operate to defeat whatever sanctions might be put into effect against Italy.

A new impulse to the debate on American neutrality in relation to sanctions of the League of Nations was given by the introduction by Senator Pittman in January, 1936, of a new bill to replace the law expiring on February 29.[20] Efforts were now made to extend the embargo provisions to include "essential war materials," such as the Administration had sought to get traders voluntarily to refrain from exporting in October and November of the previous year. Some went so far as to propose that all trade beyond the pre-war levels of a five-year average should be embargoed. Senator Pittman limited his own proposal to giving the President the power to restrict to the pre war level the export to a belligerent country of "certain articles or materials used in the manufacture of arms, ammunition or implements of war or in the conduct of war" (Sec. 4), provided the President thought such restrictions would serve to promote the security and preserve the neutrality of the United States or to protect the lives and commerce of its nationals, as in the case of the discretionary sections of the act of 1935, with the addition, "or that to refrain from placing

THE ACT OF 1936

---

[18] Department of State, *Press Releases*, XIII, 338 (November 2, 1935).
[19] *Ibid*, 382 (November 16, 1935).
[20] Senate Bill 3474, 74th Congress, 2d Session.

38 such restrictions would contribute to a prolongation or expansion of the war."

This section of the bill was strongly supported by the co-operationists, who, however, would have gone further and given the executive the authority to remove the embargo on behalf of the victim of aggression "as soon as he has determined, in consultation with other states, who is the aggressor." Equally determined opposition to these new discretionary powers resulted in the withdrawal of the entire bill, and a new and shorter one was adopted amending certain terms of the act of 1935, extending the operation of the embargo on arms to May 1, 1937, and adding two new sections.[21] The first of these new provisions made it unlawful for any person within the United States to "purchase, sell, or exchange bonds, securities, or other obligations of the government of any belligerent country" issued after the date of the proclamation of a state of war, or to "make any loan or extend any credit to any such government" or person acting on its behalf. This provision of the law, in the eyes of its proponents, now put restraints upon the bankers, who for profits might lure the country into war, similar to the restraints already put upon the munitions makers. The second of the new provisions was that the act should not apply "to an American republic or republics engaged in war against a non-American state or states, provided the American republic is not cooperating with a non-American state or states in such war." This was, indeed, from a legal point of view an extraordinary proposition; for it committed the United States to a definitely discriminatory policy without reference to the character of the war in which the American republic might be engaged, save only that it should not be acting in its character as a member of the League of Nations. The explanation is

[21] The Joint Resolution was approved February 29, 1936. For the text, see Francis Deák and Philip C. Jessup, *op. cit.*, II, 1105.

doubtless to be found in the fact that an attack upon an Amer-
ican state would immediately bring into play the Monroe
Doctrine; and apparently Congress was confident that the
American republic would not itself be the one to start a war.

In January, 1937, a new issue arose which cut across the
lines of the cooperationists and the isolationists and had the
effect of confusing the whole issue of neutrality in relation
to the prevention of war. Technically the revolution in Spain
was a civil war, a domestic problem to which the ordinary
rules of neutrality did not apply. Actually, in consequence of
assistance given by the Soviet Government to the "Loyalists"
and by the Italian and German Governments to General
Franco, the Spanish civil war soon took on an international
character. By a joint resolution, approved January 8, 1937,
Congress made it unlawful, "during the existence of the state
of civil strife now obtaining in Spain," to export arms, ammunition, or implements of war to Spain or to another country
for transshipment to Spain.[22] The resolution clearly did not
come under the head of "neutrality" legislation; and it was
sharply criticized by those who were sympathetic with the cause
of the Loyalist government, believed to be hurt the more by
the embargo. Considered, however, as legislation designed, as
it was, primarily to prevent the possible involvement of the
United States in a situation which threatened at any time to
develop into a general international war, the resolution seems
fully justified.[23] International law has as yet not developed any
rules regulating civil war; [24] so that, with the Non-Interven-

[22] For the text, see Francis Deák and Philip C. Jessup, *op. cit.*, II, 1143.

[23] For a discussion of the problems of international law involved in the
Spanish civil war, see Norman J. Padelford, *International Law and Diplomacy in the Spanish Civil Strife* (1939).

[24] See, on this point, C. G. Fenwick, "Can Civil Wars be Brought under
the Control of International Law?" *Am. Journal of Int. Law*, XXXII
(1938), 538.

tion Committee in London seeking to prevent the spread of the conflict, there was every reason why the United States should refrain from taking sides, which the shipment of arms would have tended to bring about.

Early in 1937, as the date for the expiration of the joint resolution of 1936 approached, the struggle began once more between those who would formulate the new law so that it might have a preventive effect upon the outbreak of war and those who sought to isolate the United States even more from involvement. Again the issue turned chiefly upon whether the President should be given "discretionary power," which would leave him some degree of freedom in the application of the law. But whether the President was to have more discretion or less, the terms of the proposed legislation were to be far more comprehensive. The darker the clouds of war in Europe the more public opinion seemed to demand that no occasion should be given in another war for a repetition of the "incidents" which had helped to create the war spirit in 1917. If the "freedom of the seas," that is, the defense of neutral rights of intercourse and trade, was contributory to the entrance of the United States into the World War, better abandon the freedom of the seas and keep American ships at home. If the American ownership of goods in transit to a belligerent port meant that Americans would have an interest in the goods until they reached their destination, better prevent that interest by making it unlawful to export them until "all right, title, and interest" in them should have been transferred to some foreign government, corporation, or national which might take the risk instead.[25]

[25] It was apparently an oversight which required "cash" in the case of "any articles or materials whatever" that might be exported, yet forbade the carriage in American ships of only those "certain materials or articles" which might be placed by the President on the additional embargo list. This was corrected in the law of 1939.

Thus was developed the "cash and carry" plan: the goods
must be paid for before leaving the United States and they
must be carried in some one else's vessels, it did not matter
whose.[26] The goods were defined as "certain articles and materials in addition to arms, ammunition and implements of war,"
according as the President should find that restrictions upon
their shipment were necessary "to promote the security or preserve the peace of the United States or to protect the lives of
citizens of the United States." The discretion left to the President was, therefore, limited to determining the need for restrictions on these articles; it did not carry with it any power to
discriminate against one belligerent in favor of the other. In
view of the highly controversial character of this section of the
proposed legislation it was provided that it should not be effective after May 1, 1939.

Other new provisions made it unlawful to "solicit or receive
any contribution" for a belligerent government, extended the
discretionary power of the President to exclude from American
ports not only submarines but armed merchantmen, made it
unlawful for American citizens to travel on vessels of the belligerents, where previously it had been at the risk of the traveler,
and made it unlawful for an American vessel engaged in commerce with a belligerent state to be armed or to carry armament. For the rest the new law continued the mandatory arms
embargo of the earlier law, the prohibition against the sale of
bonds or the making of loans, the prohibition against the use
of American ports as a base of supply, and other provisions of
the earlier act. The new law was approved May 1, 1937.[27]

[26] It should be noted that the "cash" part of the so-called "cash and
carry" plan does not mean "no credit," but merely no ownership of the
goods after they leave the United States. The prohibition against making
loans or extending credits comes in the next section (3) of the law.

[27] For the text of the law, see Francis Deák and Philip C. Jessup, *op. cit.*,
II, 1106.

When hearings before the Senate and House Committees on Foreign Relations and Foreign Affairs began in the spring of 1939, conditions in Europe had come to the verge of war. The "cash and carry" section (2a;2b) of the act of 1937 was about to expire by time limitation. Once more, those who believed that a definite discriminatory policy by the United States against "treaty breakers" might yet serve as a warning against further aggression sought to amend the law along those lines. Senator Thomas of Utah introduced a resolution to amend section 2 of the act by a blanket provision making it unlawful to export "certain articles or materials of use in war," as named in the President's proclamation, to belligerent states; but this was followed by a new section (3A) providing that whenever the President should find that a state signatory to a treaty to which the United States was a party was engaged in war with another state in violation of such treaty, he might, with the approval of a majority of each House of Congress, "exempt such other state, in whole or in part," from the provisions of the embargo, provided the other state was not itself engaged in war in violation of the treaty.[28] Inasmuch as the "articles or materials of use in war" would undoubtedly include oil, copper, scrap iron, and other essential raw materials of war industries, it was believed that the passage of the resolution would have a far greater deterrent effect than the discriminatory arms embargoes which the same groups of persons had previously supported.[29] Among those supporting the resolution was a group which had long sought to restrain the flow of war materials to Japan, which, they urged, made the United States

[28] For the text of the Thomas Resolution, see Senate Joint Resolution 67, 76th Congress, 1st session.

[29] Chief support for the resolution came from a group of associations organized as "The American Union for Concerted Peace Efforts."

an accomplice in the devastation wrought by the Japanese armies in China.[30]

Other resolutions before the two committees varied all the way from mandatory "cash and carry" plans for articles or materials of whatever kind to the outright repeal of the acts of 1935, 1936, and 1937 and a return to the traditional rules of international law as interpreted by the executive department of the Government. Senator Pittman, Chairman of the Foreign Relations Committee, introduced a resolution described as the "Peace Act of 1939," [31] in which the distinction between "arms, ammunition and implements of war" and other "articles or materials" was abandoned, and the "cash and carry" plan was applied to "any articles and materials." The Pittman resolution also gave to the President the power to define "areas of combat operations" through which it should be unlawful for citizens or vessels of the United States to proceed. The argument made for the Pittman resolution, the principle of which received the support of the State Department on May 27, was that there was no substantial reason for the distinction between munitions of war and the raw materials from which they were made, and that the important thing was to keep American citizens, their property, and their ships out of the danger zones. Debate on the numerous resolutions wore on for months. On July 14 the President urged prompt action in accordance with an attached statement of the Secretary of State.[32] Congress, however, adjourned on August 4 without reaching a conclusion.[33]

[30] The American Committee for Non-Participation in Japanese Aggression.

[31] For the text, see Senate Joint Resolution 97, 76th Congress, 1st Session. The name describes the purpose of the bill far better than "Neutrality Act."

[32] For the text of this important statement, see Department of State *Bulletin,* July 15, 1939, p. 43.

[33] Upon receiving word from Senate leaders that no action on neutrality legislation could be obtained at that session, it was stated in a press release from the White House, July 18, that, "The President and the Secretary of

The declaration of war by Great Britain against Germany on September 3 brought a realization of the urgent need of legislation. A proclamation was promptly issued by the President on September 5, bringing into effect the provisions of the act of 1937.[34] Inasmuch as the "cash and carry" plan was no longer in effect, having expired on May 1 by its own time limits, it was realized generally that the way was open for the creation of new "incidents" which might bring on serious controversies with the belligerents. In consequence the President on September 13 summoned Congress in special session, and on September 21 delivered a message [35] in which he urged that the embargo provisions of the act of 1937 be repealed as being "wholly inconsistent with ancient precepts of the law of nations." Repeal of the embargo on arms, he said, would put the country "back on the solid footing of real and traditional neutrality." In place of the embargo on arms the President stated that the government would insist that "American citizens and American ships keep away from the immediate perils of the actual zones of conflict"; and he proceeded to outline a bill along the lines of the one he had advocated in July.

Congress was now where it was two months earlier, except that there was no longer any question of the effect which the legislation might have in preventing war, but rather of its effect

---

State maintained the definite position that failure by the Senate to take action now would weaken the leadership of the United States in exercising its potent influence in the cause of preserving peace among other nations in the event of a new crisis arising in Europe between now and next January." The new crisis unhappily arose a month later.

[34] For the text of the proclamation, see Appendix A. The proclamation is to be distinguished from another of the same date which brought into effect the provisions of the Penal Code of 1909 relating to the duties of the United States as a neutral under international law. See below, p. 115, No. 22.

[35] For the text of the message, see Department of State *Bulletin,* September 23, 1939, p. 275.

in helping to keep the country out of a war which it was now
too late to prevent. The imperative thing, as a large majority
saw it, was to prohibit such contacts with the belligerents as
might create anew the conditions that led to war in 1917, and
for this purpose some form of "cash and carry plan" was
needed. Such a plan could, in fact, have been adopted without
lifting the embargo on arms. But those groups in and out of
Congress which previously favored using the embargo as a
means of restraining potential aggression were now in favor of
lifting the embargo because to do so would clearly assist those
who were restraining actual aggression. While the President,
in his message to Congress, had argued solely on grounds of a
return to international law and long-established national policy, it was not difficult to read between the lines of his message
his own personal attitude. Phrases like: "acts of aggression,"
"by April new tensions," "further acts of military conquest,"
"new threats of conquest," and particularly the statement that
the embargo provisions "had the effect of putting land powers
on the same footing as naval powers" and that "a land power
which threatened war could thus feel assured in advance that
any prospective sea-power antagonist would be weakened
through denial of its ancient right to buy anything anywhere"
clearly indicated where the President believed responsibility
for the war to lie and what he believed the practical effect of
lifting the embargo would be.

The debate in the Senate will always be of historic importance, even though there were few new arguments to be made.
To the opponents of the President's appeal it seemed as if the
lifting of the embargo would be an open invitation to the country to take sides in the war. Once more we were on the road of
1917; the lesson of the World War seemed to have taught us
nothing. The technical argument was made that it was in violation of neutrality to make a change in neutrality legislation

in time of war.[36] There were, however, numerous precedents in favor of imposing and raising embargoes in time of foreign war, as the Embargo and Non-Intercourse Acts during the Napoleonic wars. These, however, were said to have been enacted from the right motive of protecting the interests of the United States, whereas the present proposal to lift the embargo on arms was from the wrong motive of helping the Allies.[37] The argument on law thus got lost in the argument on motives, which were in truth the determining factors; but such was the spell which "neutrality" had cast over the country that only a few Congressmen were bold enough to admit that behind technical neutrality was an actual desire not to handicap Great Britain and France in a war for which Germany was believed to be responsible.

THE
"NEUTRAL-
ITY ACT
OF 1939"

The Joint Resolution, approved November 4, 1939, is to be cited as the "Neutrality Act of 1939." [38] It calls attention in its

[36] On this controversial question, see C. G. Fenwick, "The Revision of Neutrality Legislation in Time of Foreign War," *Am. Journal of Int. Law,* XXXIII (1939), 728; letters by Charles Cheney Hyde and Philip C. Jessup and by Clyde Eagleton, *The New York Times,* September 21 and 25; October 5 and 15, 1939. A World War precedent was found in the statement of Secretary Bryan on April 21, 1915, in answer to the complaints of Germany about the shipment of arms from the United States, that "any change in its [the United States Government's] own laws of neutrality during the progress of a war which would affect unequally the relations of the United States with the nations at war would be an unjustifiable departure from the principle of strict neutrality." But in this case there was the question of changing a long-established rule in favor of a new one, whereas the reverse was the case in 1939.

[37] The "cash and carry" plan, enacted at the same time with the lifting of the embargo on arms, operated clearly to the advantage of Germany. But no objection was raised to it by the opponents of revision in time of war, since, it was said, its purpose was primarily to protect the interests of the United States. On the other hand it might be said that the lifting of the embargo balanced the imposition of the cash and carry plan.

[38] The name is unfortunate. Senator Pittman's "Peace Act of 1939" was

preamble to the fact that the United States, desiring to preserve its neutrality and to avoid entanglement in foreign wars
"voluntarily imposes upon its nationals" the restrictions to follow, but in so doing "waives none of its own rights and privileges, or those of any of its nationals, under international law."
The act then proceeds to provide that it shall be "unlawful for
any American vessel to carry any passengers or any articles or
materials" to a state named in the President's proclamation as
being at war; further, that it shall be unlawful to export "any"
articles or materials until all right, title, and interest therein
should have been transferred to some foreign government,
agency, or national. The act thus sets up a "cash and carry"
plan for arms as well as for the "certain other articles or materials" contemplated in the act of 1937. Inasmuch as Canada
was a belligerent and there could be no danger of "incidents"
in connection with trade over the border, the act made exception of transportation by American vessels or aircraft on inland waters or over lands bordering on the United States; and
provision was further made that the act should not apply to
transportation by American vessels or aircraft to ports in the
Western Hemisphere south and west of fixed lines or to ports
on the Pacific or Indian oceans, thus excluding Australia, New
Zealand, South Africa, and other parts of the British Empire
from the operation of the prohibitions against trade in American vessels. The President was given power, if he found that
the protection of American citizens so required, to define "combat areas" through which it should thereafter be unlawful for
American citizens or vessels to proceed. For the rest the act
followed the lines of the earlier act of 1937. Promptly upon his
approval of the act the President issued a proclamation bring-

---

possibly thought to sound inappropriate with a war actually in progress.
"National Security Act" would have fitted better, or "Keep Out of War Act"
even better. For the text of the act, see Appendix B.

48   ing it into effect and revoking his earlier proclamations which had given effect to the act of 1937.

Thus came to an end the long struggle between those who had advocated and those who had opposed changes in the traditional policy of the United States with the object of preventing war by denying to a treaty-breaking state access to the economic resources of the United States. Now that war had actually come, public opinion in overwhelming majority found but one course to follow—to keep out of it. It remained then, and it still remains to be seen whether "neutrality legislation" of any kind could give an assurance of that. For behind all such legislation must be the will of the American people to remain neutral, and that will must of necessity be dependent upon an estimate of the degree to which the national interests of the United States are adversely affected as the war proceeds. It is the curse of war that it tends to draw one nation after another into its vortex, and that it may come to affect vitally the national interests of those who, though desiring earnestly to avoid it, have nevertheless failed to take preventive measures against it.

IV. NEUTRAL RIGHTS

It is an unhappy comment upon the civilization of western Europe that the development of international law from the sixteenth century onwards should have consisted chiefly in the elaboration of the law of war. War was a legal procedure; the best that the international lawyers could do was to try to restrain the belligerents. Vitoria and Grotius appealed to them on moral grounds.[1] Later writers laid stress upon the customs that had come to be regarded as having the force of law. But each succeeding treatise that came from the hand of diplomat or of scholar gave chief place to what was or what was not lawful in warfare.[2] It is significant that, of the thirteen conventions adopted at the Hague "Peace" Conference of 1907, eleven related to the conduct of the next war, which the statesmen at the Conference naïvely imagined would be fought according to the rules which they were preparing for it.

CONFLICT
BETWEEN
NEUTRAL
AND BEL-
LIGERENT
RIGHTS

[1] In publishing his famous treatise in 1625, Grotius announced that his reason for doing so was that he "saw prevailing throughout the Christian world a license in making war of which even barbarous nations would have been ashamed; recourse being had to arms for slight reasons or for no reason; and when arms were once taken up, all reverence for divine and human law was thrown away, just as if men were thenceforth authorized to commit all crimes without restraint." *De jure belli et pacis,* Whewell's translation, Prolegomena, §28 (Cambridge University Press, 1853).

[2] It is interesting to note that such standard treatises as those of John Westlake, L. F. L. Oppenheim, and Thomas J. Lawrence classified the two main branches of international law as the "law of peace" and the "law of war."

In the development of this "law of war" the conflict between the "rights of the belligerents" and the "rights of neutrals" played a leading part. War, as we have seen, was a legal procedure. A state, finding itself unable to secure recognition of its claims or redress for its alleged wrongs, took the law into its own hands. When it did so it automatically acquired certain "rights" not only with respect to the conduct of military and naval operations against the enemy, but with respect to the commercial intercourse of neutral states with the enemy. The primary purpose of the belligerent was to win the war. To do that he was prepared to go to any lengths. He would fight the enemy on land and on the high seas; he would destroy his commerce at whatever inconvenience to third states; he would carry the war up to the very edge of neutral territory; he would himself make every permissible use of neutral resources, while indifferent to the effect of his hostilities upon the normal economic life of the neutral. He was as lawless as the "law" of war would permit him to be.

It was to be expected that neutral states on their part would seek to hold the belligerents within the strict limits of what the traditional law allowed them, and indeed to narrow those limits as far as possible. The struggle was a long one, and, as we have seen, by the time of the Hague Conference of 1907 the neutrals had succeeded in winning respect for their claims. If belligerents had rights, so had neutrals. The *rights* of the one naturally implied *duties* on the part of the other. From the very nature of war it was to be expected that the precise dividing line between the two sets of rights and duties would not be clear. But at the close of the Hague Conference it seemed as if the conflict between belligerent and neutral claims had been brought sufficiently under regulation to permit neutrals to stay neutral without sacrifice of their rights. The World War dispelled that illusion; and it is clear that the present war will mark the surrender of neutral rights to belligerent demands in even greater degree.

The most vital right of a neutral state is the protection of its neutral territory against acts of war on the part of the belligerents. Here the sovereignty of the neutral state is involved, and there can be no compromise with either belligerent.[3] For the neutral to yield its rights in favor of one belligerent would be guilty of a gross violation of neutral duty to the other. "The territory of neutral states is inviolable," said the Hague Convention of 1907.[4] The belligerent must "respect the sovereign rights of neutral Powers" and must abstain "from any act which would, if knowingly permitted by any Power, constitute a violation of neutrality." [5] The rule is strictly interpreted. Not only would an open battle fought upon neutral territory be a violation of neutral sovereignty, but lesser acts of hostilities, such as the passage of belligerent troops across neutral territory, come equally under the ban. The neutral may, indeed, not be in a position to resist the commission of hostilities. Belgium undertook to do so in 1914, and it came under the German yoke for the duration of the war. Luxemburg yielded without a struggle. China looked on helpless while Japan fought for the possession of the German lease on the tip of the Shantung peninsula. But the inability of the neutral to resist does not lessen in any degree the inviolability of its territory or the belligerent duty to respect it.

[3] A sort of magic has come to surround the word "sovereignty," as if the very life of the nation depended upon it and even the smallest state, if it is to survive in a lawless world, must make its final stand there. Incidentally the conception of sovereignty has done as much as anything else to defeat the effort to organize the community of nations for the mutual protection of those very things that sovereignty is supposed to represent.

[4] Convention (V) Respecting the Rights and Duties of Neutral Powers and Persons in War on Land.

[5] Convention (XIII) Concerning the Rights and Duties of Neutral Powers in Naval War.

The United States, from the time of its growth in size and power, has escaped the fate of weaker neutrals. Only a few incidents can be found to mark the violation of its territory or its territorial waters. In 1793 a French privateer captured a British vessel, the *Grange,* within the waters of Delaware Bay. Secretary Jefferson, acting upon an opinion of the Attorney-General that the waters were territorial, demanded the release of the prize. The French Minister, Genêt, admitting the illegality of the capture, released the vessel.[6] In the case of the *Anna,* in 1805, the British Court of Admiralty released a Spanish vessel captured by a British privateer near the mouth of the Mississippi River. The affair might have been of more consequence had it not been for the fact that the capture was made outside the three-mile limit if measured from the mainland, but within it if measured from some small mud islands off the coast.[7]

Case of the "Florida" But if the United States has not suffered as a neutral from the violation of its territorial sovereignty it has itself been guilty as a belligerent of violating the sovereignty of neutrals. In 1864, during the American Civil War, the United States warship *Wachusett* captured the Confederate cruiser *Florida*

[6] *American State Papers, Foreign Relations,* I, 147 ff.; John Bassett Moore, *A Digest of International Law,* I, §153.

[7] C. G. Fenwick, *Cases on International Law* (1935), p. 450. In the well-known case of the *Caroline,* the Canadian government, during the progress of a rebellion in 1837, sought to anticipate an attack upon its territory and dispatched a force across the Niagara River to a point on the American side from which the insurgents were obtaining supplies, capturing and destroying the vessel and killing two of the crew in the act. Inasmuch as the insurgents had not been recognized as belligerents the case does not come properly under the head of violations of neutrality. It is interesting chiefly because of the classic statement made by Secretary Webster that, in order to justify the action of the Canadian authorities, the necessity of self-defense should be "instant, overwhelming, and leaving no choice of means, and no moment for deliberation."

in the territorial waters of Brazil. Due apology was made for an act which, it was admitted, was "unlawful and indefensible." But inasmuch as the *Florida* had foundered in Hampton Roads it could not be restored to Brazil, and the Confederate "raider," as it would now be described, was thus conveniently disposed of.[8] In like manner the United States, by formal disclaimer of the capture of the *Chesapeake* in British territorial waters off Nova Scotia in 1865, disposed of a vessel that had earlier been captured by persons acting in the interest of the Confederacy.[9]

Does the broad right of self-defense justify a belligerent in resisting attack by the enemy in neutral territorial waters? In 1814 the American privateer *General Armstrong* defended itself against the attack of a British squadron in Portuguese waters; and the United States not only considered the defense justifiable, but brought a claim against Portugal for damages for failure to give protection.[10]

The "General Armstrong"

What extenuating circumstances might be found for an attack by one belligerent against another in neutral territorial waters? In March, 1915, two British cruisers attacked the German warship *Dresden* within the territorial waters of Chile. The British foreign office promptly apologized; but at the same time it offered in explanation the fact that the *Dresden* itself was abusing the neutrality of Chile by a pretense of internment behind which it was seeking an opportunity to commence hostilities anew.[11]

"The Dresden"

More spectacular is the recent case of the German auxiliary transport *Altmark* which, on February 16, was attacked by a

Case of the "Altmark"

[8] For details of this historic incident, see John Bassett Moore, *op. cit.,* VII, 1090; C. G. Fenwick, *Cases on International Law,* p. 743.

[9] John Bassett Moore, *op. cit.,* II, §210.

[10] C. G. Fenwick, *Cases on International Law,* p. 750. See below, p. 102.

[11] See James W. Garner, *International Law and the World War* (1920), II, §562.

54   British cruiser in Norwegian territorial waters. On board the *Altmark* were some three hundred British officers and men belonging to various British merchant vessels which had been captured and sunk by the German warship *Graf Spee*. Having released the prisoners the British cruiser left the *Altmark* to the disposal of those of its crew who remained on board after the encounter.

The Norwegian Government promptly presented "a strong protest" against the illegal act of the British cruiser.[12] Foreign Minister Koht, in a statement before the Norwegian Parliament on February 19, insisted that as the *Altmark* was a "state ship" it was not bound to submit to search and in consequence the Norwegian patrol boats were not guilty of neglect of neutral duty. The *Altmark*, it was said, "had all rights to navigate through Norwegian territory. . . . There is no rule at all forbidding a war power to transport prisoners through a neutral area, in so far as navigation itself is not illegal." The following day the British Prime Minister made a statement before the House of Commons in which he criticized the failure of the Norwegian authorities to conduct a search of the vessel in spite of the fact that it had been "prominently reported weeks ago in the press of the world" that there were prisoners on board and in spite of the request of the British cruiser that a search be conducted. The Prime Minister then took exception to the view of the Norwegian Government that such use as the *Altmark* had made of the territorial waters of Norway was within the rules of international law; and going further he attacked the general practice of the Norwegian Government in permitting the German warship to make use of Norwegian waters "for hundreds of miles" as a means of escaping capture.[13]

[12] So described in the excerpts from the address of Foreign Minister Halvdan Koht. *The New York Times,* February 20, 1940, p. 4.

[13] The issue on this point came to a head with the laying of mines by the

Three distinct issues seem to be presented by the case. In the
first place, did the *Altmark* violate the neutrality of Norwegian
territorial waters? The answer would seem to be in the affirma-
tive. For it would be admitted that the seizure of the prisoners
in Norwegian waters, if for example they had been adrift in
open boats, would be an act of hostility; and there is no substantial difference, so far as concerns the use of force by one
belligerent against another which constitutes "hostilities," between the forcible seizure of the prisoners and their forcible detention in the hold of the prison ship.[14]

Was Norway delinquent in its neutral duty? It would seem
not, so far as the specific case of the *Altmark* was concerned.[15]
For the Norwegian Government could not be expected to give
heed to British press reports; and there appears to have been
no formal request from the British Government for a special
investigation. If the vessel's papers indicated correctly that it
was a public ship it was normally immune from search. Norway's redress for the fact that there were actually prisoners on
board would be through diplomatic channels after the fact had
been discovered from other sources.

British Government in the territorial waters of Norway, and the prompt occupation of Norwegian ports by German troops. See below, p. 103.

[14] The American case of the *Sitka* has been cited against this position. But
the *Sitka* forms an unconvincing precedent, being merely the opinion, mis-
taken, as the writer sees it, of an Attorney-General in a case involving two
or three prisoners on board a British vessel which stopped in the harbor of
San Francisco en route to its home port.

It should be observed that not until the World War did the practice, still
technically illegal, develop of holding the crew of captured enemy merchant
vessels as prisoners of war. The Hague Convention (XI) of 1907 provided
that they should not be made prisoners if they gave a written promise not to
engage in any service connected with the operations of war.

[15] The question whether the general right of a neutral state to permit
"freedom of passage" through its territorial waters can be made to cover the
use by German vessels of the long stretch of the Norwegian coast line is discussed later under the head of "Neutral Duties." See below, p. 103.

56   What, then, of the alleged justification by Great Britain of the conduct of its cruiser in committing hostilities in Norwegian waters? The case must be defended, if at all, upon the doctrine of self-defense. The normal procedure for the British Government should have been to call upon the Norwegian Government to demand of the German Government the return of the prisoners to Norway on ground of their illegal transport through Norwegian waters, assuming that Great Britain could have convinced Norway of the illegality of the transportation. But the British Government was doubtless well aware that there was, as a practical matter, small hope that any such request from Norway would be heeded by the German Government. Hence the orders to the British cruiser *Cossack* to secure the release of the prisoners before it was too late.

RESTRIC-
TIONS
UPON BEL-
LIGERENT
USE OF
NEUTRAL
PORTS

Not only has the neutral state the right to protect its territory against the actual commission of hostilities by belligerents, but it has the further right to prevent its territory from being made a base of belligerent operations against the enemy. Here the *right* of the neutral against both belligerents relates to situations which it is generally found more convenient to discuss in terms of the *duty* of the neutral to the belligerent which may be injured by the failure of the neutral to enforce its rights.[16] As in the case of the *Altmark,* just discussed, the same facts may raise a question of neutral right, belligerent right, and neutral duty, according to which of the parties is making the complaint.

*Exclusion
of sub-
marines*

Has a neutral state the right to exclude belligerent warships and auxiliaries from its ports and territorial waters? While the right has been questioned, it would seem that it is supported

[16] There is, unfortunately, no accepted classification of neutral rights and duties. The textbooks upon the subject vary in their analyses of the problem; and the various international conventions have been drafted along lines of convenience rather than of logic.

both by logic and by practice.[17] Few states, however, have felt
it necessary to go so far as to exclude all belligerent warships.
But many have believed it desirable to exclude submarines.
Here the motive has doubtless been not only to prevent the
violation by submarines of local regulations in respect to stay
in port, but to express the general policy of the neutral state
in respect to those instruments of warfare from which neutrals
have suffered so severely.[18] In pursuance of the authority conferred by the Joint Resolution of 1937 President Roosevelt issued a proclamation on October 18, 1939, making it unlawful
for any submarine of the belligerent nations "to enter ports or
territorial waters of the United States," except only in cases of
force majeure. A number of other American states likewise undertook to exclude them. On February 2, 1940, the Inter-American Neutrality Committee, acting upon an inquiry addressed
to it by the Government of Uruguay, presented to the American Republics a Recommendation in which were offered the
alternative policies (a) of exclusion from ports, harbors, or
territorial waters, subject to cases of *force majeure,* or (b) of
admission, subject to prescribed conditions of navigation and,
in the case of entrance into ports or harbors, subject to the

[17] At the Hague Conference of 1907 it was agreed merely that a neutral
power "must apply impartially to the two belligerents" the conditions fixed
by it for admission to its ports. The reference in the Convention (XIII)
was rather to neutral duty than to neutral right; and the reporter of the
committee stated, in reply to an inquiry, that "the right" of a state to forbid
access to its ports was not in question, that following from its right to issue
general regulations and prohibitions (A. Pearce Higgins, *The Hague Peace
Conferences,* p. 467). The Harvard Draft Convention on Rights and Duties
of Neutral States in Naval and Aerial War contains an article (26) accepting the general right of exclusion; and, in the Comment upon this article,
the belief is expressed that it "lays down an existing rule of international
law."

[18] The controversy between the United States and Germany over the use
of the submarine against merchant shipping is discussed below, p. 63.

necessity of obtaining special permission from the neutral government in each particular case.[19]

While there is no question of the general right of the neutral state to regulate the privileges which may be granted to belligerent warships and auxiliaries in its ports, provided of course that equal treatment be accorded to both sides, controversies have arisen occasionally in respect to the abuse of those privileges. Here the neutral is asserting its rights chiefly in order to perform its neutral duty. In December, 1914, for example, the United States Department of State refused clearance papers to German merchant vessels carrying supplies to German warships on the ground that the repeated departure of the vessels made the port a base of naval operations for the belligerent; and again, in March, 1915, the United States requested the British Government to prevent the recurrence of "violations of the territorial waters of the United States" by British cruisers taking on coal and other supplies along the coast of California.[20]

On December 13, 1939, the German pocket battleship *Graf Spee*, following a battle with three British cruisers, took refuge in the harbor of Montevideo. The Uruguayan Government, intent upon maintaining its rights as a neutral and fulfilling its duties, decided that the necessary repairs to make the vessel seaworthy could be made within seventy-two hours; and, over

[19] In the preamble to the Recommendation it is said that the majority of the Committee considered it desirable to recommend the exclusion of submarines from neutral ports and harbors, "being led to that conclusion not only by the difficulties attending the regulation of the activities of submarines but by a desire to give expression in that manner to the universal reprobation of the use of submarines as commerce destroyers; nevertheless, the Committee should take into account the practical circumstances confronting the adoption of a rule of strict exclusion of submarines." For the text of the Recommendation, see *Pan American Union, Law and Treaty Series,* No. 13, Supp.

[20] *American White Book,* II, 33.

the protests of the German commander, ordered the vessel to leave port at the end of that period.[21] The vessel steamed out of the harbor on the afternoon of December 17 and, after its officers and crew had been transferred by prearrangement to the German merchant ship *Tacoma*, was scuttled at a point in the river about six or seven miles off shore.[22] The officers and crew, transferred later from the *Tacoma* to smaller vessels, proceeded to Buenos Aires, where they were interned by the Argentine Government.[23] The *Tacoma* proceeded back to Montevideo, where it was itself interned by the Uruguayan Government.[24]

What is the status of armed merchant ships of the belligerents in neutral ports? Are they to be accorded the unrestricted privileges of ordinary merchant ships or must they be held to the limited privileges fixed by international law for warships. The issue has been a highly controversial one. In so far, however, as regards the *right* of the neutral to prescribe either status for them, there would seem to be no room for doubt. The question of neutral *duty* in the matter, which was raised by Germany at the beginning of the World War, soon became subordinated to the larger question of the legality of submarine

[21] The Uruguayan Government is greatly to be commended for the courage and decision with which Foreign Minister Guani and other officers acted on that occasion.

[22] An interesting question might be raised whether the scuttling of a warship in neutral territorial waters should be regarded as an act of "hostilities," or at any rate as a trespass upon the territory of the neutral state. After its suicidal act the vessel continued to lie in the bed of the river, a menace to local traffic. But the Government of Uruguay did not press a claim on this account, and acquiesced in the sale by the German Government to a local contractor of the right to remove the derelict vessel.

[23] On the question of internment of the officers and crew of the *Graf Spee*, see below, p. 110.

[24] For the treatment of the *Tacoma* for its illegal conduct in assisting the *Graf Spee*, see below, p. 113.

warfare, and it is more convenient to discuss it in that connection.

PROTEC-
TION OF
CITIZENS
ON THE
HIGH
SEAS

Passing from the right of the neutral state to protect its territory against the operations of war, whether open hostilities or lesser violations, we come to the issue which the United States made the technical ground of its entrance into the World War. Has a neutral state the right to protect its citizens when traveling on belligerent merchant ships, whether armed or unarmed? Has the neutral the right to protect them when traveling on vessels of other neutrals? Has it the right to protect vessels of its own nationality against attack if, in spite of warning from the belligerents, they enter war zones proclaimed by the belligerents to be areas of unrestricted warfare? The three problems all converged upon the formidable issue presented early in 1915 by the appearance of the German submarine as a destroyer of enemy commerce. The older rules of international law had developed in relation to conditions which did not include this new instrument of warfare. Not a single provision of the Hague Conventions of 1907 had anticipated it.

We may begin with the attitude of the United States towards armed merchant vessels of the belligerents in its ports when the question was presented in the opening month of the war. Great Britain had announced that certain of her merchant vessels entering American ports would be armed, but that their armament would be used solely for purposes of defense, so that the vessels should be entitled under international law to enjoy in neutral ports the status of peaceful trading ships. Germany on its side promptly protested the fact that an armed British liner, the *Adriatic,* had been allowed to stay in port more than twenty-four hours. On September 19, 1914, the United States Department of State issued a circular in which it was announced that a merchant vessel of belligerent nationality might carry armament "for the sole purpose of defense" without acquiring the character of a ship of war. The presence of 61 armament, it was said, created a presumption that the armament was for "offensive purposes," but this presumption might be overcome by evidence of defensive purpose only. Such evidence was to consist in the number, size, and position of the guns, together with other factors in relation to the commercial destination of the vessel and the character of its cargo.[25] In taking this position the Department had in mind the traditional right of a belligerent merchant ship to defend itself against privateers,[26] and the fact that British merchant ships would now have to face the danger of being attacked by German merchant ships converted into warships after the outbreak of the war.[27]

Early in October Great Britain announced that, in consequence of the German practice of laying mines, "certain areas" of its own had been defined which it would be "dangerous henceforward" for neutral ships to cross.[28] A month later the

War zones

[25] *Papers Relating to the Foreign Relations of the United States,* 1914, Supp., 611.

[26] The early case of the *Nereide* (9 Cranch 388) was frequently referred to. Here Chief Justice Marshall had stated that "a belligerent merchant vessel rarely sails unarmed" and that it had a "perfect right" to arm in its own defense, but that in doing so it became "an open and declared belligerent." See C. G. Fenwick, *Cases on International Law,* pp. 757, 795.

[27] The Hague Convention (VII) Relating to the Conversion of Merchant Ships into Warships, 1907, had fixed the conditions under which such change of character might take place.

[28] At the Hague Conference of 1907 an earnest effort was made by the British delegate to have the Conference adopt a rigid prohibition against the laying of automatic contact mines on the high seas. The German delegate was prominent in opposition. The result was that the Convention (VIII) Relative to the Laying of Automatic Submarine Contact Mines adopted an evasive prohibition that: "It is forbidden to lay automatic contact mines off the coasts and ports of the enemy, with the sole object of intercepting commercial navigation." A. Pearce Higgins, *The Hague Peace Conferences,* p. 328. The Harvard Draft (see above, p. 57, n. 17) allows mines to be sown in a "blockade zone," but not on the high seas indiscriminately.

British Admiralty announced that the whole of the North Sea must be considered a "military area," and that all ships entering the area would do so "at their own peril." This was followed on February 4, 1915, by a statement from the German Government that in retaliation for British violations of international law, including the North Sea war zone, Germany now declared "all the waters surrounding Great Britain and Ireland including the entire English channel as an area of war" and would endeavor to destroy all enemy merchant vessels found in that area "without its always being possible to avert the peril, that thus threatens persons and cargoes." Neutrals were therefore "warned" against entrusting passengers and goods to such ships; and their attention was called that it was "advisable for their own ships to avoid entering this area" because, in view of the misuse of neutral flags by the British Government and other contingencies of naval warfare, they might become victims of torpedoes directed against enemy ships.

A strong reply to the German Government was sent on February 10.[29] Secretary Bryan reminded the German Government that the sole right of the belligerent in respect to neutral vessels on the high seas was limited to visit and search, unless an effective blockade was being maintained; that it would be an act "unprecedented" in naval warfare to attack a vessel without ascertaining by visit and search its nationality and the character of its cargo; that to destroy on the high seas "an American vessel or the lives of American citizens" upon the mere presumption that the flag of the United States was not

[29] The documentary history of the negotiations may be found in the *American White Book*, I-IV; *Papers Relating to the Foreign Relations of the United States*, 1914-1917; or, in more compact form, in Carlton Savage, *Policy of the United States toward Maritime Commerce in War* (Washington: Government Printing Office 1934-1936), II, 50-51.

being used in good faith would be regarded by the United States as an "indefensible violation of neutral rights," for which the United States would hold the German Government to "a strict accountability" and would "take any steps" that might be necessary to safeguard American lives and property on the high seas.[30]

Thus was the legal basis laid for the controversy which was to follow. Matters soon came to a head. On March 28 the British ship *Falaba* was sunk by a submarine in the zone delimited by the German note of February 4, one American citizen being reported lost in consequence of the short time given to those on board to escape after the vessel heeded the warning to stop. The President was of the opinion that what had been done was "in unquestionable violation of the just rules of international law." Secretary Bryan was of the opinion that account should be taken of the fact that "the deceased knowingly took the risk." Before a reply could be agreed upon the tragic sinking of the *Lusitania* had taken place on May 7, involving a loss of one hundred twenty-eight American lives.

The negotiations with Germany which now began were long and complicated. The formal note of protest sent by Secretary Bryan to Germany on May 13 was, in spite of popular excitement attending the tragedy, restrained in tone. It called attention to the earlier note that the United States would hold Germany to "strict accountability" for infringement of American rights; it assumed that Germany accepted the principle that the lives of noncombatants should not be jeopardized by the destruction of an "unarmed" merchantman; it insisted upon the belligerent obligation of visit and search; and it drew the conclusion that, in view of the practical conditions attending their use, submarines could not be used against

[30] Carlton Savage, *op. cit.*, II, 265.

64   merchant ships without "an inevitable violation of many sacred principles of justice and humanity." The fact that warnings had been issued, in the form of advertisements in the daily press, could not be accepted as an excuse for the commission of an "unlawful and inhuman" act. The act must be disavowed, reparation made, and steps taken to "prevent the recurrence of anything so obviously subversive of the principles of warfare" for which Germany had in the past contended.[31]

The German position   The German Government replied on May 28, and a series of replies and counter-replies followed. In substance the German contention was that the *Lusitania* was not in the class of an "ordinary unarmed merchant vessel but was in the class of an auxiliary cruiser, that it was armed,[32] and that on previous trips it had carried Canadian troops and large quantities of ammunition." Moreover, the general practice of the British Government in arming its merchant ships and instructing them to use neutral flags and to attack the enemy made it impossible to consider them any longer as "undefended territory" in the zone of maritime warfare. In addition, the unlawful blockade of Germany and the unwarranted extension of the rules of contraband made it necessary to resort to reprisals. As against the German position Secretary Lansing, in a note of June 9, waived aside the arguments based upon the conduct of Great Britain and insisted that the United States was "contending for nothing less high and sacred than the rights of humanity" and that only the "actual resistance [of the Lusitania] to capture or refusal to stop when ordered to do so for the purpose of visit could have afforded the commander of the submarine any justification for so much as putting the lives of those on board the ship in jeopardy." Once more he reiterated the

[31] Carlton Savage, *op. cit.*, II, 315, 317.
[32] On the question of its alleged armament, see *The Lusitania*, 251 Fed. 715 (1918) ; C. G. Fenwick, *Cases on International Law*, p. 731.

principle that "the Government of the United States cannot admit that the proclamation of a war zone from which neutral ships have been warned to keep away may be made to operate as in any degree an abbreviation of the rights either of American shipmasters or of American citizens bound on lawful errands as passengers on merchant ships of belligerent nationality." In a third note of July 21 Secretary Lansing argued against the German justification of retaliation for the conduct of Great Britain; and, in reply to the argument that allowance should be made for the use of instrumentalities (the submarine) which the nations did not have in view when the existing rules of international law were formulated, he asserted that "the rights of neutrals in time of war are based upon principle, not upon expediency, and the principles are immutable. It is the duty and obligation of belligerents to find a way to adapt the new circumstances to them."

Thus the controversy reached a deadlock. The United States wanted a definite acknowledgment that Germany recognized the attack upon the *Lusitania* as "unlawful." This the German Government would not give. The furthest it went, in a note of May 4, 1916, a year after the sinking of the *Lusitania,* was to agree that both within and without the zone merchant vessels "shall not be sunk without warning and without saving human lives, unless these ships attempt to escape or offer resistance," but that neutrals could not expect that for their sake Germany should "restrict the use of an effective weapon if her enemy is permitted to continue to apply at will methods of warfare violating the rules of international law.[33] To this Secretary Lansing replied that "respect by German naval authorities for the rights of citizens of the United States upon the high seas should [not] in any way or in the slightest degree be made contingent upon the conduct of any other government affecting

[33] *American White Book*, III, 302 ff.

the rights of neutrals and noncombatants. Responsibility in such matters is single, not joint; absolute, not relative." [34]

Throughout the controversy it does not appear there was any thought in President Wilson's mind of asking Congress to pass a law forbidding American citizens from traveling on vessels of the belligerents and American vessels from entering the designated war zones. After the sinking of the *Falaba* Secretary Bryan was of the opinion that the "doctrine of contributory negligence" had some bearing upon the case, in that an American who took passage upon a British vessel knowing the kind of warfare that would be employed stood "in a different position" from one who suffered without any fault of his own.[35] After the sinking of the *Lusitania* Secretary Bryan again raised the point, suggesting that those who took passage on the *Lusitania* had done so in a measure at their own peril, and therefore were "not entitled to the full protection" of the government. This position was opposed by Counselor Lansing, who was supported by President Wilson on the ground that, even though a warning might have operated as an exemption from the responsibility of the government to protect its citizens, it was now too late to take that position. "We defined our position at the outset," the President held, "and cannot alter it,—at any rate so far as it affects the past." [36] The question of a warning to American citizens against travel on belligerent ships seems to have been discussed at this time solely in connection with the responsibility of the Government to press a demand against Germany for redress. A few days later Counselor Lansing prepared, at the request of Secretary Bryan, a draft of a public notice, to be issued by the President requesting American citizens to refrain from taking passage on bel-

[34] Carlton Savage, *op. cit.*, II, 494.
[35] *Ibid.*, II, 289.
[36] *Ibid.*, II, 314.

ligerent vessels pending the negotiations with Germany over the use of submarines. But no notice was then issued.

The following year when the Gore-McLemore Resolutions, warning American citizens against traveling upon armed merchantmen of the belligerents, were under consideration, the President made known his opposition, taking the ground that to forbid the American people to exercise their rights "for fear we might be called upon to vindicate them" would be "an implicit, all but an explicit, acquiescence in the violation of the rights of mankind everywhere, and of whatever nation or allegiance." [37] There was the issue, clearly defined. American citizens could have been warned that their government would not have protected them if they took the risk of traveling on armed merchant ships of the belligerents; they might even have been prohibited by law from doing so. But a principle was at stake: to surrender to lawlessness would, as the President saw it, be a denial of everything the United States had stood for. The resolutions failed of passage.

In spite of the rigid position taken by the State Department in the *Lusitania* case in its refusal to consider the justification of changes in the traditional law due to "new circumstances," the Department recognized in the fall of 1915 that its regulations issued in September, 1914, with respect to the status of armed merchant vessels, might have to be modified to take account of the obvious difficulty of reconciling the alleged "defensive" armament of British merchant ships with the vulnerability of the submarine when appearing upon the surface to give the customary warning before attack.[38] For a year the

New proposals on armed merchant ships

[37] *Ibid.,* II, 461.

[38] In the protest made over the sinking of the *Lusitania* reference had been made to the unlawful destruction of an "unarmed merchantman," as was in fact the case with that vessel. The Department of State seems to have regretted later that the negotiations with Germany had been conducted on that restricted basis.

68   British Admiralty kept guns off British merchant vessels entering American ports. Now they were arming them. What was to be done about it? In a communication of September 12, 1915, to President Wilson, Secretary Lansing explained that at the time the declaration of September 19, 1914, was issued the "use of the submarine as a commerce destroyer was unknown, and declaration was based on the means employed prior to that time." "I feel in my own mind," said the Secretary, "that these changed conditions require a new declaration because an armament, which under previous conditions, was clearly defensive, may now be employed for offensive operations against so small and unarmored a craft as a submarine." [39]

It was not until January 18, 1916, that Secretary Lansing submitted, in identic notes to the Entente Governments, his compromise proposal for bringing to an end the "dangers to life" which attended the use of submarines as destroyers of commerce on the high seas, his interest in the matter being not the neutrality of American ports but the fact that American citizens, "in the exercise of their recognized rights as neutrals" might be passengers on such vessels or members of their crews.[40] The belligerents were to agree that submarines on their part should adhere strictly to the rules of international law in stopping and searching merchant vessels, determining their belligerent nationality, and removing passengers and crew to a place of safety before sinking the vessels as prize of war; while merchant vessels of the belligerents "should be prohibited and prevented from carrying any armament whatsoever." The argument in support of the proposal was based upon the fact that the customary right of a merchant ship to go armed was "predicated upon the superior defensive strength

[39] Carlton Savage, op. cit., II, 384.
[40] The text of this important document may be found in the American White Book, III, 162 ff.; Carlton Savage, op. cit., II, 441.

of ships of war" and the relatively inferior armament of pirati-
cal ships and privateers. The use of the submarine had, however, changed these relations, and moreover pirates had been
driven from the seas and privateering abolished. Hence the
arming of a merchant ship under the existing conditions could
be explained only on the ground of a purpose to make the ship
superior in force to submarines and to prevent warning and
visit and search by them. "Any armament, therefore, on a merchant ship," it was argued, "would seem to have the character
of an offensive armament."

The proposal was reported by Ambassador Page as unaccept-
able to Great Britain. The Austro-Hungarian Government
hearing indirectly of the proposal, informed Secretary Lansing
that the Central Powers were considering an announcement
that armed merchantmen would not be treated as peaceful
vessels. On February 8 the announcement was made.[41] Secretary Lansing was then in the embarrassing position of having
argued the German case and yet not wishing to exclude armed
British merchantmen from American ports without the consent
of the British Government to the new proposal. He, therefore,
issued a statement [42] explaining that, while the Government
felt that "the present rule of international law permitting belligerent merchant vessels to arm ought to be changed," nevertheless the Government did not feel that it could change or
disregard the established rule "without the assent of the contending belligerents," and would, if the Entente Powers rejected the proposal, "rely upon the present established rule
of international law" that merchant ships were entitled to

---

[41] An unpleasant personal controversy developed over the statement of
the Austro-Hungarian Chargé that Secretary Lansing had said he would
"welcome" such an announcement. For the Secretary's explanation of his
alleged statement, see Carlton Savage, op. cit., II, 465.

[42] For the text, see ibid., II, 457.

armament for defensive purposes only. The Government reserved, however, the right to change its regulations in regard to the evidence as to armament on merchant vessels arriving in American ports which would indicate that it was defensive only. The new regulations, drawn up in a memorandum of March 25,[43] were made public on April 26, 1916. In them the position was taken that the status of an armed vessel as a warship in neutral waters was to be determined on the basis of facts creating a presumption of aggressive purpose, and the status of such vessel on the high seas by conclusive evidence of aggressive purpose.

Germany
renews the
war zone

The stage was now set for the final denouement. The sinking of the *Sussex* on March 24 had led to an open threat that diplomatic relations would be broken off unless Germany immediately abandoned "its present methods of submarine warfare against passenger and freight carrying vessels." On May 4 the declaration demanded was made, but contingent upon the abandonment by Great Britain of its "methods of warfare violating the rules of international law." The attacks by submarines upon merchant ships continued. On January 10, 1917, the German Government took once more its ground of the previous year that armed merchant vessels were to be treated as "belligerents"; and on January 31 the final announcement came that after February 1 Germany would "meet the illegal measures of her enemies" by forcibly preventing, in a zone around Great Britain, France, and Italy, "all navigation, that

[43] This important memorandum represents what might be called the last stand of the Department on the controversy. See Carlton Savage, *op. cit.*, II, 487. Sharp differences of opinion have been expressed as to the correctness of the principles it asserts. See, in criticism, Charles Cheney Hyde, *International Law Chiefly as Interpreted and Applied by the United States* (1922), II §743; and in defense, James Wilford Garner, *International Law and the World War*, I, §249.

of neutrals included." All ships met within that zone would
be "sunk." [44]

Diplomatic relations between the United States and Germany were promptly severed. The President asked Congress for authority to arm American merchant vessels; but the "little group of willful men," as the President described them, prevented a vote in the Senate before the session closed on March 4. A number of American vessels were sunk by submarines. On April 2 Congress met in extra session. The President reviewed the situation.[45] The German submarine warfare against commerce was a "warfare against mankind," it was "a war against all nations." Each must decide for itself how to meet the challenge. He advised that Congress "declare the recent course of the German Imperial Government to be in fact nothing less than war against the government and people of the United States." This decision taken, the President then went on to describe the larger motives and objects which the United States must keep before it: "Our object," he said, was "to vindicate the principles of peace and justice" against selfish and autocratic power, and to set up among the really free and self-governed peoples of the world "such a concert of purpose and of action" as would henceforth ensure the observance of those principles. Neutrality was "no longer feasible or desirable" where the peace of the world was involved and the freedom of its peoples. We were at the beginning of an age in which it would be insisted that the "same standards of conduct and of responsibility for wrong done" should be observed among nations that were observed among individual citizens.

The President's address to Congress

Such is the story, in summary, of the legal aspects of the historic controversy that led up to the declaration of war by Congress on April 6, 1917. Volumes have been written of re-

Congress declares war

[44] For the text, see Carlton Savage, *op. cit.*, II, 555.
[45] For the text, see *ibid.*, II, 589.

cent years to show that there were other forces at work behind the negotiations. The bankers who had an interest in the repayment of their loans and the munitions makers who saw opportunities for vast profits are said to have developed between them such an effective control of the press that the country was swept into war by force of propaganda it could not resist. Congress is said to have yielded to popular emotion against its better judgment. The President, it is asserted, was ill-advised on points of law and was thrown off balance by his academic visions of a better ordered world.[46]

Thus has run, at great length, the propaganda against the propaganda of the war profiteers; and it will doubtless be many years before there will be any measure of agreement as to the relative weight to be given to the many forces at work. One thing, certainly, is clear, that any time President Wilson could have surrendered the "rights" for which he contended. But he did not view the surrender as many persons have been led to view it in recent years. He believed there was a larger principle at stake than the mere defense of American lives and property; that the surrender of that principle would mean a greater loss to the United States than could be measured by the sacrifices that would have to be made to maintain it.[47] The large majority in Congress that voted for war did not "want war"; but neither did they want to yield to "lawlessness." Public opinion in the country had slowly come to take sides; or rather, having taken sides from the start, it had now come to realize

[46] Possibly Edwin M. Borchard and William P. Lage, *Neutrality for the United States*, present the most effective criticism, but with avowed bias. Charles Seymour, *American Neutrality, 1914-1917*, defends the Administration; Alice M. Morrissey, *The American Defense of Neutral Rights, 1914-1917*, is critical but fair.

[47] The President's position in this respect is perhaps most strongly stated in a letter to Senator Stone, Chairman of the Committee on Foreign Relations, February 24, 1916. Carlton Savage, *op. cit.*, II, 461.

that neutrality was an impossible position to maintain, that
the United States had a vital interest in the defeat of the
country which was believed to be responsible for the war and
whose lawless conduct in the course of it seemed to indicate
what its conduct would be like if it won the war. The conception that the whole war system was wrong and that something
would have to be done about it was doubtless confined to a few
who, with the President, looked ahead to a constructive peace.[48]

In the years succeeding the World War efforts were made
to regulate the use of the submarine in the future. In a treaty
signed on February 6, 1922, at the close of the Washington
Conference on the Limitation of Armaments it was provided
that the submarine must conform to the established rules of
visit and search, and that if circumstances prevent it from
doing so it must permit the merchant vessel to proceed unmolested.[49] Moreover, in view of the practical impossibility of
using submarines as commerce destroyers without violating
the laws of war, the contracting powers prohibited as between
themselves the use of submarines for that purpose. The provisions of the Washington treaty in respect to the observance
by the submarine of the laws of war were repeated at the

[48] In all this the propaganda of the bankers, munitions makers, and business men, such as it was, played a relatively negligible part. Dr. Alice M. Morrissey, in a recent volume (*The American Defense of Neutral Rights, 1914-1917*), which is otherwise critical of the policy of the Government, summarizes the various influences as follows: "The United States went to war with Germany because it passed a moral judgment on her behavior, because it insisted upon a broad interpretation of neutral rights, and because after developing a huge economic interest on one side it lacked an economic deterrent to going to war with the other."

[49] *Treaties, Conventions, International Acts, Protocols and Agreements between the United States of America and Other Powers* (Washington: Government Printing Office, 1910-1938), III, 3116.

Renewal of
submarine
warfare

AUTOMATIC
CONTACT
MINES

Havana Convention on Maritime Neutrality of 1928 [50] and at the London treaty of 1930.[51]

Germany, however, was not a party to these agreements, and the present war is being fought with an even greater disregard of neutral rights in this respect than was the case during the World War. The reason no controversies have arisen is simply because the United States has preferred to abandon the use of the seas in the "combat areas" in which submarines are being used. What action the Government will take in the event that a submarine should attack an American vessel outside of the combat area proclaimed by the President on November 4 cannot be predicted.

Not only have the neutrals which, from necessity, are still using the high seas adjacent to the British Isles suffered severely from unrestricted submarine warfare in the present war, but they are suffering in perhaps equal degree from the indiscriminate sowing of automatic contact mines.[52] American ships have thus far escaped fatalities by avoiding the designated combat areas. Again it remains to be seen what action will be taken should the sowing of mines become even more indiscriminate and disasters occur within the areas still permitted to American vessels. The problem of mines has been raised before the Inter-American Neutrality Committee in

[50] Manley O. Hudson ed., *International Legislation; A Collection of the Texts of Multi-partite International Instruments of General Interest Beginning with the Covenant of the League of Nations* (Washington: Carnegie Endowment for International Peace, 1931-1936, 5 vols.), IV, 2401.

[51] *U. S. Treaty Series,* No. 830.

[52] The Harvard Draft (see above, p. 61, n. 28) recognizes the difficulty of securing an absolute prohibition against the laying of automatic contact mines outside of belligerent territorial waters and carries an article (83) allowing them to be sown in "blockade zones." This, however, was far from sanctioning recent German practice, which appears to have known no bounds. The casualties in Scandinavian shipping have been particularly heavy.

connection with the possible adoption of a common policy on 75 the part of the American states in respect to the protection of cargoes which cannot reach their destination except by going through the dangerous areas.

Have neutral states the right to insist upon the immunity of their citizens and property from the incidents of warfare when resident in belligerent countries? Would it make any difference in this respect whether the injuries suffered by the neutral citizens were the indirect result of lawful hostilities or were incurred in consequence of belligerent acts in violation of the laws of war? On the first of the latter points it has been the attitude of the United States that neutral residents must share the fate of the civilian population in whose midst they are living. Such was the attitude taken by Secretary Seward towards complaints of the British and French Governments during the American Civil War. But what of losses incurred as a result of lawless acts of the belligerents, such as the bombardment of unfortified towns? The difficulty in such cases is to prove the lawlessness of the belligerent acts. For unfortunately the Hague Conventions regulating belligerent conduct in time of war left many loopholes in the form of concessions to military necessity. It has not been until the present war that belligerent conduct has become so lawless as to leave no ground for doubt as to its lawlessness, as in the case of the destruction of Warsaw and other Polish towns by Germany and the parallel destruction of Helsinki and other Finnish towns by Russia. Thus far, however, the United States has taken no direct diplomatic action.[53]

[53] The destruction of neutral mails on neutral vessels sunk by illegal methods of warfare practised by Germany was cited by Great Britain, in its note of January 17, 1940, as properly calling for protest from the United States far more than the mere search of neutrals by Great Britain. See below, p. 100.

PROTECTION OF CITIZENS IN BELLIGERENT COUNTRIES

On April 22, 1940, it was announced that the American Military Attaché at Stockholm, Captain Robert M. Losey, had been killed by a German bombing plane at Dombas, Norway, while endeavoring to assist American citizens who were fleeing from the country before the German invaders. In as much as the Norwegian town was undefended, it would appear that the United States would be fully justified in holding the German Government to "strict accountability," for whatever that might be worth.

V. BLOCKADE AND CONTRABAND: THE CONFLICT OF NEUTRAL AND BELLIGERENT RIGHTS

If neutrals have found it difficult, not to say impossible, to maintain the integrity of their territory and to protect the lives of their citizens on the high seas against the efforts of the belligerents to carry on their hostilities with maximum effectiveness against each other, so too in matters of trade and commerce neutrals have felt the heavy hand of the belligerents and have been forced at times to yield reluctantly to their demands. Here also have come changes of circumstances to raise the question whether rules, worked out under one set of conditions, were to continue binding when new and unforeseen conditions arose. Here also the belligerents, with their backs to the wall and their national life at stake, have been tempted to break through the restraints that have been put upon them. Here also the neutral has on occasion been faced with the choice of defending its neutral rights by force or of abandoning them when it has thought them not worth fighting for.

The right of the belligerent to interfere with neutral commerce with the enemy has a long historical background.[1] It antedates by many hundreds of years the relatively modern conception of the obligation to respect neutral territory and the even more modern resort to ruthless methods of warfare by submarines and contact mines. Just as in warfare on land it

[1] See Philip C. Jessup and Francis Deák, *Neutrality, Its History, Economics and Law*, Vol. I.

was the custom to lay siege to fortified cities and attempt to starve them into submission, so in warfare at sea it became one of the primary objects of the belligerents to surround the ports of the enemy state and prevent it from receiving supplies from overseas. In the maintenance of such a blockade of enemy ports, or rather in the partially ineffective effort to maintain it, the belligerent came into direct conflict with the trade of neutrals. In consequence the history of maritime war is in large part a history of the controversies between belligerents on the one side seeking to prevent the access of neutral shipping to enemy ports and on the other side neutrals seeking to protect the trade of their citizens as far as possible by holding the belligerents down to the strict limits of the practices recognized by customary law as properly within their lawful rights.

Blockades to be binding must be effective

The first and fundamental rule in regard to a blockade is that it must be a real blockade. It will not do for a belligerent merely to draw a line around the enemy coast line and declare that it is blockaded, and then proceed to capture neutral vessels destined to one or other of the ports included within the line. War simply does not confer such a right upon the belligerent. It must either maintain an effective blockade or none at all. Putting the case graphically, it might be said that if the belligerent cannot capture more than one ship in ten, it cannot capture any at all. The rule may seem to lack logic, but it has a historical basis in the fact that neutrals have succeeded in resisting any claim on the part of the belligerent to cut off their trade with the enemy by mere arbitrary fiat; and therefore it is incumbent upon the belligerent either to maintain an effective blockade or to limit his interference with neutral trade to the capture of contraband of war.

The acceptance of this rule in the Declaration of Paris of 1856 following the Crimean War came only after long controversy between belligerents and neutrals. The Armed Neutralities of 1780 and 1800 directed their protests in part against blockades legally established but not effectively maintained. In the Russian declaration of 1780, which formed the basis of the Armed Neutrality of that year, it was said that "as to what concerns a port blocked up, we ought not, in truth, to consider as such any but those which are found so well shut up by a fixed and sufficient number of vessels, belonging to the power which attacks it that one can not attempt to enter into such port without evident danger." [2] The Congress of the United States approved of the Russian declaration and would have acceded to the Armed Neutrality had it not been limited to neutrals. The principle of the Russian declaration was adopted by Congress in its "Treaty Plan of 1784"; [3] it was included in the instructions to John Jay in 1794, and it became thereafter the established policy of the United States.

Controversies leading to the war of 1812

The story of the long and complicated controversies in which the United States was involved with Great Britain and France following the renewal of war between them in 1803 is now of historic interest only, being, in respect to the legal problems at issue, superseded by the controversies raised during the World War. It is the story of the young republic seeking, as Jefferson described it, to maintain an "honest neutrality," but being unable to do so because the belligerents would not let it. In addition to the issues of blockade and contraband there was the dispute over the impressment by Great Britain of seamen of alleged British nationality when the latter were found on American vessels during the course of belligerent visit and search. Which of the three issues was the dominant one in building up the public sentiment that supported the declaration of war in 1812 it would be difficult to tell. Perhaps the quite ir-

[2] Carlton Savage, *Policy of the United States Toward Maritime Commerce in War*, I, 140.
[3] *Ibid.*, I, 157.

relevant object of redressing grievances by annexing Canada must explain the final decision of Congress to resort to war.[4]

In respect to the issue of illegal blockades the controversy began with the British Order in Council of May 16, 1806, which set up a blockade in two distinct zones, one between the Seine and Ostend, which was absolute, the other, outside these limits, applicable to vessels trading between France and her colonies. But before the United States could protest on the ground of the ineffectiveness of the latter blockade, Napoleon issued his Berlin decree of November 21, 1806.[5] While the French justification of this decree was retaliation for what was described as England's blockade of places "before which she has not a single vessel of war," the French retaliatory blockade had even less justification in point of effectiveness than the British blockade. Great Britain retaliated in turn with an Order in Council of November 11, 1807, which declared a blockade of all European ports from which British ships were excluded. Napoleon retaliated with his Milan decree of December 17, 1807, which ordered the seizure of all vessels submitting to British search or touching at British ports.[6]

What were neutral American vessels to do, caught as they were between the illegal measures of both belligerents? President Jefferson, anxious to avoid provocations for war and believing that it was better for American ships to remain at home than to risk almost certain capture, recommended to Congress

[4] On this point, see Samuel F. Bemis, *A Diplomatic History of the United States* (1936), p. 156.

[5] The curious feature of this decree was that it not only declared that the British Islands were in a state of blockade (which Napoleon was powerless to enforce), but it also denied access to continental ports, which Napoleon controlled, of all vessels trading in British goods or coming from British ports. This latter feature was essentially a "self-blockade."

[6] Details may be found in the books of John H. Latané, Samuel F. Bemis, and other standard histories of American foreign policy.

that an embargo be put on American commerce, making illegal the departure of American vessels for foreign ports. The act was passed on December 22, 1807,[7] and it met with indignant protest in New England. Better the loss of a few vessels, it was argued, than be cut off from the profits of a lucrative if dangerous trade. So unpopular was the embargo that it was repealed before the end of Jefferson's term, but out of deference to him was not made effective until March 15, 1809. Jefferson had asked the American people to pay too high a price to be kept out of war, and they were unwilling to pay it!

Congress was willing, however, to cut off trade with the two offenders, and on March 1, 1809, an act was passed to prohibit commercial intercourse with Great Britain and France and their dependencies, at the same time authorizing the President to reestablish intercourse with whichever of the belligerents should first suspend its edicts.[8] This act was repealed on May 1, 1810, and in its place the President was authorized, in case either Great Britain or France should withdraw its orders, to prohibit commerce with other. Napoleon now misled President Madison into believing that the offending French decrees had been withdrawn; and as a result the President proclaimed that the nonintercourse act was in effect against Great Britain. This as confirmed by a new non-intercourse act of March 2, 1811, directed against Great Britain only. Great Britain, doubting the genuineness of the French repeal but feeling the pressure of the non-intercourse act, revoked its orders in council on June 23, 1812. In the meantime, however, the problem of impressment

The Non-Intercourse Acts of 1809, 1810 and 1811

[7] For the text, see Francis Deák and Philip C. Jessup, *A Collection of Neutrality Laws, in Various Countries*, II, 1120.

[8] For the text, see Francis Deák and Philip C. Jessup, *op. cit.*, II, 1161. The discriminatory character of this embargo was clearly intended to permit the President to bargain with the belligerents.

had become acute; and Congress, responding to a message of President Madison on June 1, had declared war on June 18.[9]

In 1856, at the close of the Crimean War, the Declaration of Paris formally announced the rule that "blockades, in order to be binding, must be effective; that is to say, maintained by a force sufficient really to prevent access to the coast of the enemy." The principle was now definitely established; but it remained to be seen whether the definition of an effective blockade offered a rule sufficiently precise to be applied to specific cases.[10]

During the American Civil War new conditions confronted the vessels of the United States blockading the coasts of the Confederate States. This time, however, the United States was a belligerent and its interpretation of an "effective" blockade was naturally less restrictive. New doctrines were found to meet the new conditions. British merchant vessels, planning to run the blockade, found it convenient to use British neutral ports in the Bahamas as stopping places en route to a Confed-

[9] While the question of impressment figured more prominently in the President's message than that of the illegal blockades, the latter case was stated in strong terms: "Under pretended blockades," said President Madison, "without the presence of an adequate force and sometimes without the practicability of applying one, our commerce has been plundered in every sea, the great staples of our country have been cut off from their legitimate markets, and a destructive blow aimed at our agricultural and maritime interests. . . . And to render the outrage the more signal these mock blockades have been reiterated . . . in the face of official communications from the British Government declaring as the true definition of a legal blockade 'that particular ports must be actually invested and previous warning given to vessels bound to them not to enter.' " J. D. Richardson, *A Compilation of the Messages and Papers of the Presidents, 1789-1897*, (Washington: Government Printing Office, 1896), I, 499.

[10] The Declaration of London of 1909, repeating the rule, added that the question whether a blockade was "effective" was a question of fact. Inasmuch, however, as this question of "fact" had to be decided by the prize court of the belligerent which captured the neutral vessel for breach of blockade, there was still room for controversy.

erate port. Was it lawful to capture them on their way from
London or Liverpool to the neutral port used as a stopping
place? The United States applied to such cases the doctrine of
"continuous voyage" applied earlier by Great Britain to prohibited colonial trade.[11] Moreover, the further and more important innovation was introduced of distinguishing between
the destination of the vessel and the destination of the cargo,
so as to meet the case where the vessel itself had a bona fide
neutral destination, but the cargo was to be transshipped to a
smaller and swifter vessel which would have a better chance of
running the blockade. This new rule came to be known as the
doctrine of "continuous transports." In the leading case of the
Springbok,[12] the Supreme Court of the United States condemned the cargo of a British vessel captured en route to the
neutral port of Nassau on the ground that the character of the
cargo was such as to indicate that its owners intended that it
should be transshipped at Nassau to a smaller vessel which
might have a better chance of breaking the blockade.

The precedent created by *The Springbok* returned to haunt
the United States when it was its turn to be a neutral in 1914-
1917. The conditions were somewhat different from those of
1861-1865, inasmuch as Great Britain was now seeking to
capture ships destined to neutral European ports whose cargoes would, on arrival at the neutral port, be sent on by land
to Germany. The Declaration of London had repudiated the

*Continuous
transports
during the
World War*

---

[11] This was the famous "Rule of 1756." It was involved in the famous
case of the *Essex*, in which the British prize court had condemned an American vessel on the ground that the mere stopping at a neutral port did not
break the continuity of the voyage from an enemy colony to the enemy
homeland. See, on this subject, John Bassett Moore, *A Digest of International Law*, VII, 383; Herbert Whittaker Briggs, *The Doctrine of Continuous Voyage* (Baltimore: The Johns Hopkins Press, 1926).

[12] 5 Wallace 1 (1866); C. G. Fenwick, *Cases on International Law*, p. 763;
Carlton Savage, *op. cit.*, I, 460.

doctrine of *The Springbok*. But the Declaration was not binding; and Great Britain, by way of retaliation for the war zone declared by Germany on February 4, 1915, announced on its part, on March 11, that not only vessels of enemy destination would be required to discharge their goods in a British port, but that even vessels of neutral destination might be required to do the same. The question at issue now was whether the new British blockade was in violation of the accepted rule, confirmed in the Declaration of London, that a blockade must not extend beyond the ports and coasts belonging to the enemy and must not bar access to neutral ports or coasts. The United States had refrained from blockading the Rio Grande in 1861-1865, in spite of the fact that traffic between Mexico and the Confederate States across the river made evasions of the regular blockade readily possible. But modern communications by rail and motor transport had changed the situation in Europe, so that it was one and the same to Germany whether the supplies came direct to its own ports or indirectly through neutral ports.

Blockade of neutral countries

In reply to the British Order in Council of March 11 the United States, on March 30, set forth at length its views on the new form of blockade which, it was said, amounted to "a practical assertion of unlimited belligerent rights over neutral commerce within the whole European area." [13] The "unprecedented feature" of the blockade was that it embraced "many neutral ports and coasts," barred access to them, and subjected neutral (American) ships seeking to approach them to the same suspicion as if they were bound to enemy ports. The Government of the United States was, the note said, "not oblivious to the great changes which have occurred in the conditions and means of naval warfare since the rules hitherto governing legal block-

[13] The text of this important note may be found in Carlton Savage, *op. cit.*, II, 281.

ade were formulated. It might be ready to admit that the old form of 'close' blockade with its cordon of ships in the immediate offing of the blockaded ports is no longer practicable in the face of an enemy possessing the means and the opportunity to make an effective defense by the use of submarines, mines, and aircraft; but it can hardly be maintained that, whatever form of effective blockade may be made use of, it is impossible to conform at least to the spirit and principles of the established rules of war." The note then urged that it was "easily practicable" to accord "free admission and exit to all lawful traffic with neutral ports through the blockading cordon."

To this elaborate and, it would seem, legally convincing argument the British Government, on July 24, pointed out in reply that the neutral countries adjacent to Germany afforded her convenient opportunities for trade with foreign countries and that a blockade limited to enemy ports "would leave open routes by which all kinds of German commerce could pass almost as easily as through the ports in her own territory." If, it was said, the United States might, when a belligerent during the Civil War, intercept goods destined for enemy territory before they reached the neutral ports from which they were to be reexported,[14] was it unfair for Great Britain to pursue the same methods when the second stage of the journey was by land?

It was clear by this time that the argument could not be settled on the basis of law. The Civil War precedents cited by Great Britain were in truth not strictly applicable. For in both of the leading cases, *The Springbok* and the *Peterhoff*, the United States had confined its seizures to goods that were absolute contraband and had not condemned goods that were destined to the open market of the neutral adjacent to the enemy. But, *New conditions, new rules*

[14] The reference was to cases similar to that of *The Springbok*. See above, p. 82.

on the other hand, they were sufficiently applicable to make out a good case if allowance was to be made for the change of circumstances due to modern transportation; and just as the United States in creating the precedents cited by Great Britain had itself gone beyond the existing law to meet new conditions, so Britain could claim to be doing the same thing. The problem was further complicated by the fact that the British Government sought to evade the charge that its blockade extended to neutral ports and coasts by justifying its seizures by a liberal interpretation of the law of contraband. Here the field for controversy, as we shall see, was wide and open.

The extension of blockade to exports

During the present war Great Britain has extended still further its blockade of Germany by seeking not only to prevent *imports* into the country, but to prevent *exports* from it as well. The theory behind these new restrictions is that if Germany can be prevented from selling goods abroad it will be unable to obtain the exchange necessary to buy goods from other nations, even from nations bordering on Germany. Thus the blockade against exports is an indirect way of preventing imports, and in that respect it operates against imports even from countries adjacent to Germany which could not be reached by the British sea blockade. On November 28, 1939, Great Britain, by Order in Council, undertook to intercept all ships and all goods coming from German ports or ports in occupation by Germany and all ships from whatever port sailing after December 4 having on board goods of German origin or German ownership, and to require that the goods be discharged in a British or Allied port.

To this order the United States vigorously protested in a note released December 8, in which it was argued that interference by belligerents with neutral shipping was, under the rules of international law, strictly limited to breach of blockade and capture of contraband, under neither of which heads

the announced order to seize exports from Germany could be
brought. Moreover, the note urged, there were practical reasons for protest against the order, among which was the fact that in many instances the goods had already been paid for and in other instances the goods could not be duplicated in other markets, thus causing losses to the American purchaser who needed the goods in his industry or his profession.[15] Subsequently it was suggested by the British Government that exceptions might be made in cases in which there was special need by the American importer of the goods in question, and that "assurances" of non-interference with such consignments would be given.[16]

The right of a belligerent to intercept neutral goods of a CONTRA-
military character on their way to the enemy was, in the early BAND
days of international law, only another application of the right
to maintain blockade. Both were means by which a belligerent
sought to isolate the enemy, and the capture of contraband
goods was merely an extension of the scope of blockade beyond
the particular ports that were being invested. Here, as in the
case of blockade, we find the belligerents seeking to break
through the restrictions imposed by established law when those
restrictions fail to take account of the changing conditions of
the times. On the other hand we find neutrals determined to

[15] For the text of the note, see Department of State *Bulletin*, December 9, 1939, p. 651.

[16] *Ibid.*, January 6, p. 5. On March 4, 1940, the Government of Italy entered a strong protest against a recent British communication in accordance with which every ship loaded with coal leaving German ports after March 1 would be subject to control measures. The order of November 28 was described as being in violation of international law, and the gravity of the situation was emphasized by the statement that the coal in question represented "an immutable necessity to the life and work of the Italian people." As to the last point it was natural for the British to observe that their coal would burn as well as German coal.

resist belligerent practices contrary to established law, all the more so because the closely integrated commercial relationships of the nations in modern times have made neutrals feel far more severely the disruptive effects of war between two great powers than was the case even fifty years ago.

The tradi-
tional
classification
The acute issue between neutrals and belligerents involves the question, what articles come properly under the head of "contraband" and are therefore subject to capture and confiscation by the belligerent when destined to the enemy. Grotius sought to answer the question in 1625 by drawing up a threefold classification of goods, which later become the basis of British and American doctrine down to the time of the World War. In the first place there were articles of such an obviously military character that there could be no doubt as to their intended use. These were "absolute" contraband, and subject to capture without question. Secondly, there were articles which were useful both for military and for peaceful purposes. These were "conditional" contraband, the condition being that their destination must be to the military or naval forces of the enemy. Thirdly, there were articles which were not susceptible to use in war. These formed a "free" list, and they were exempt from capture as such, although they might be condemned if the vessel carrying them was guilty of breach of blockade or if the greater part of its cargo was contraband.

Changing
conditions
It was hardly to be expected that lists of goods drawn up in the seventeenth and eighteenth centuries should continue to be recognized by belligerents, notably by Great Britain as the dominant sea power, in the nineteenth century. But more remarkable still was the naïve attempt at the London Naval Conference of 1908-1909, to draw up new classifications at a time when science was already forecasting the invention of substitutes for everything short of air and water. The Declaration of London had, in addition to raw cotton and wool, put rubber

on the "free list," little realizing the uses to which rubber would
be put in automobile transport; and as if almost to invite its
own violation it also included metallic ores in the same list.
Even had the Declaration been ratified after its signature, there
is little doubt that it would have been set aside by Great Britain before the World War had been in progress many months.

The distinction between absolute and conditional contra- *Absolute*
band had been developed in the days of sailing vessels when *and con-*
goods, such as foodstuffs, remained in the port of delivery. In *ditional*
the leading case of the *Jonge Margaretha,* decided in 1799, a *contraband*
cargo of cheeses captured on its way to Brest, at that time a
French port of naval equipment, was condemned as contraband
because destined obviously for the use of the armed forces of
the enemy. Had the same cargo been destined to "a general
commercial port," said the court, it would have been exempt
from capture as being intended for "civil use." There was no
question at this time of inland transportation from a purely
commercial port to a port of naval equipment or to armed
forces operating in the interior of the country. If goods were
not to be used where they landed by the military forces they
were not to be used by them at all.

During the American Civil War the question of the destina- *American*
tion of contraband goods played an important part in deter- *Civil War*
mining the legality of the capture of contraband goods on the *doctrines*
way to neutral British and Mexican ports under circumstances
indicating subsequent enemy destination. The doctrines of
"continuous voyage" and of "continuous transports," the latter
being known also as the doctrine of "ultimate destination,"
were developed by the United States Supreme Court to meet
cases similar to those arising under the rules of blockade; for
neutral ports adjacent to the coast of the Confederate States
were being used as stopping places to disguise the true destina-

tion of the goods.[17] In the leading case of the *Peterhoff* [18] the Supreme Court condemned part of the cargo of a vessel captured en route to Matamoros, Mexico, on the ground that the evident destination of the military goods carried by the vessel was the Confederate States across the Rio Grande River. These new doctrines were attacked at the time, but they subsequently obtained recognition in the Declaration of London, where it was provided that it was immaterial in the case of absolute contraband whether the carriage of the goods was direct or entailed transshipment or a subsequent transport by land.[19] On the question of conditional contraband, however, the Declaration provided that such goods should not be liable to capture except when found on board a vessel bound for enemy territory or the armed forces of the enemy and when they were not to be discharged in an intervening neutral port.

World War changes   The outbreak of the World War showed how impractical it was not only to attempt to draw up a "free list" containing such essential raw materials as cotton, wool, rubber, and metallic ores, but to attempt to distinguish between absolute and conditional contraband on the basis of the military or civilian uses to which the goods were to be put. Germany was a manufacturing country which, if it could get the necessary raw materials, could manufacture its own munitions of war. Scarcely more than a month had gone by before Great Britain began transferring articles from the free list of the Declaration of London to the contraband list, and from the classification of

[17] On this important problem, see Herbert Whittaker Briggs, *The Doctrine of Continuous Voyage.*

[18] 5 Wallace 28 (1866); C. G. Fenwick, *Cases on International Law,* p. 767; Carlton Savage, *op. cit.,* I, 466.

[19] In the Civil War cases the question at issue was primarily the destination of the goods and not their intrinsic character, inasmuch as what the Confederate States wanted was manufactured war materials, about the character of which there could be little doubt.

conditional to that of absolute contraband. Since the Declara- 91
tion was not in force, the matter had to be decided on the basis
of customary international law.[20] Unwrought copper presented
a problem, and Secretary Bryan found "some embarrassment"
in dealing with the problem in view of the fact that the United
States had in the past placed "all articles from which ammunition is manufactured" in its contraband list.[21] He also found it
necessary to yield on the point of having petroleum products
proclaimed as contraband, "in view of the absolute necessity of
such products to the use of submarines, aeroplanes and motors."
The ball was now rolling, and cotton, at first left on the free
list, lost that status by August, 1915. Turpentine and rosin
caused a controversy, but the outcome was the same. By October 15 of that year things had reached the point where all
that Secretary Lansing could do was to argue the case on principle and to affirm that there was no intention of committing
the Government of the United States to a policy of "waiving
any objections" it might entertain as to the inclusion in the
British contraband list of "certain articles" which had been so
included. We would have something to say about it all later
on.[22]

[20] At the beginning of the World War the United States had proposed to
the belligerents that the Declaration of London be regarded as in force although it had not been ratified by the signatory powers. Germany and Aus-
tria-Hungary assented, subject to a like observance by Great Britain and
France. Great Britain adopted the Declaration with certain modifications
and additions; but the United States insisted that the provisions of the Declaration must, as stipulated by Article 65, be treated as a whole, and did not
consider that the qualified adoption by Great Britain constituted an acceptance of its proposal.

[21] Carlton Savage, op. cit., II, 247.

[22] For the text of this important document, see Carlton Savage, op. cit., II,
390. There was a fine flourish to the note about the "task of championing
the integrity of neutral rights" which the United States "unhesitatingly" assumed. The task has since been unhesitatingly abandoned.

Conditional
contraband
becomes
absolute

The problem
of foodstuffs

More controversial during the World War than the question whether particular articles might be transferred from the free list to the contraband list was the question whether the traditional distinction between conditional and absolute contraband should continue to hold in the face of the changed conditions of inland transportation. The problem was closely associated with the doctrine of ultimate destination as applied to blockade; and, as we have seen, Great Britain operated the two forms of control so that the law of contraband could be used to fill in any gaps in the law of blockade.

Promptly upon the outbreak of the war Secretary Bryan announced that under the rules of international law grain could be shipped to a belligerent country unless it was intended for the use of the army or navy or destined to a blockaded port or a port occupied by armed forces. On September 26, 1914, it was again insisted that foodstuffs were legitimate articles of commerce, and that mere destination to an enemy port did not justify their seizure or condemnation.[23] This was, indeed, a position difficult to maintain under modern conditions of transportation, for which it would seem allowance must of necessity be made. So far as Germany was concerned it was not of the slightest consequence whether the particular port at which the foodstuffs arrived was or was not occupied by its armed forces. The ultimate use of the foodstuffs would be determined by other considerations.

But a more fundamental change had taken place than the mere development of inland railways and motor transportation. That change was in the relations between the civilian population and the armed forces of the belligerent state.[24] During the

[23] For the text, see Carlton Savage, *op. cit.*, II, 197. The policy of the United States in respect to contraband in general was set forth in a public circular of August 15, 1914 (*ibid.*, II, 189).

[24] See, on this general subject, C. G. Fenwick, *International Law* (1934),

early part of the nineteenth century a number of writers put
forth the thesis that war was a relation between states as such,
not between the populations of the two countries; so that persons in the belligerent states who were not members of the
actual fighting forces were not to be regarded as enemies. This
principle, as such, never had any legal validity, but it did have
an indirect influence upon the development of the laws of war.
While the Hague Conferences of 1899 and 1907 clearly recognized that the inhabitants of a belligerent state must bear the
burdens of war as well as its organized armies, the conventions
there adopted sought to spare the civilian populations as much
as possible. It remained for the World War to demonstrate
that the outcome of the war was no longer merely a question
of the most powerful forces at a particular moment, but depended in large part upon the organized participation of the
unarmed population in the manufacture of munitions and in
other services directly contributory to the support of the armies in the field. If that was the case it made little difference
to a belligerent whether food supplies bound to a port of the
enemy were intended for the armed forces of the enemy or for
the civilian population. By April 13, 1916, Great Britain, having tried less effective measures, went to the length of abolish-
ing altogether the distinction between absolute and conditional
contraband, offering as justification the fact that so large a
proportion of the inhabitants of the enemy country was taking
part, directly or indirectly, in the war that the distinction between the armed forces and the civilian population lacked re-
ality. Moreover, the fact that the German government had

---

pp. 450-452. An interesting precedent for the identification of a belligerent
army with the civilian population may be found in the British Minister's
argument to Secretary Jefferson in 1793, when reference was made to the
fact that the French Government was aiming the laboring classes. See John
Bassett Moore, *A Digest of International Law*, VII, §1253.

taken over the distribution of articles on the list of conditional contraband and was obviously meeting first the needs of the army made the distinction between the two classes of goods meaningless. All that Secretary Lansing could now do was to notify the British Government of the "reservation of all rights of the United States or its citizens" in respect to any interests that might be adversely affected.[25]

Rationing neutral countries The "rationing" of neutral countries was a logical development, if an unwarranted one. As previously applied, the doctrine of "continuous transports" or the doctrine of "ultimate destination" did not condemn goods which were to be sold in the open market of the neutral port. Yet it soon became clear that even a guarantee from the neutral states adjacent to Germany was not enough to satisfy Great Britain. The larger the volume of foodstuffs and other supplies which neutral merchants could import, the larger the quantity of domestic produce that could be spared for overland shipment to Germany. In consequence Great Britain undertook to determine what were the normal imports of the neutral countries in time of peace and to hold them to the same average quantity in time of war. Whatever was in excess of that amount must be presumed to reach Germany by way of substitution. Every extra egg or pound of butter imported into Holland, for example, made it possible for the Dutch to export to Germany an additional egg and an additional pound of butter out of their own domestic supply. The neutrals were thus put on "rations," and what was in effect a complete blockade of Germany was established. It was done, however, not by application of the rules governing

[25] Carlton Savage, *op. cit.*, II, 532. The trouble about "reserving" your neutral rights is that either you can't make out a good enough case in point of law to get damages, or else you get into the war yourself and do things just as bad and then haven't the face to demand redress for what you suffered as a neutral.

blockade, but by an extended operation of the doctrines of con-
traband. It is interesting to note that in spite of the protests of the United States while still a neutral against the new application by Great Britain of the doctrine of continuous transports, once the United States itself became a belligerent it set upon a plan of licensing trade with neutrals which was to all intents and purposes only another form of the rationing system.[26]

Upon the outbreak of the present war the British Government promptly issued schedules of absolute and of conditional contraband.[27] In keeping with the practice of the World War, the schedule of absolute contraband contained not only arms and the raw materials and machinery necessary to their manufacture, but also fuel, contrivances for transportation, including machinery for manufacture, all means of communication and articles necessary to their manufacture, coin, bullion, currency and evidences of debt. The conditional contraband list was limited to foodstuffs and to clothing and articles and materials used in their production. The conditional list suggested that there was no present intention on the part of the British Government to regard food destined to Germany by way of non-blockaded ports as subject to confiscation on the theory of the identification of the civilian population with the armed forces. It was not long, however, before food destined to Germany came under the same absolute prohibition to which it was subject during the World War.

During the World War a system of "navicerts" was developed *The navicert* by the British Admiralty in accordance with which neutral *system* shippers might avoid the delays incident to visit and search in British control ports. In the opening months of the war the United States had held that belligerents should make their

[26] See Carlton Savage, *op. cit.*, II, 101.
[27] Department of State *Bulletin*, September 16, 1939, p. 250.

search of neutral vessels on the high seas at the time of visit.[28] This, however, proved to be a difficult position to maintain, in view of the length of time required for the search of large merchant vessels. Search in port, however, frequently involved long delays. In consequence, a plan was worked out by which American shippers might apply to the British Embassy in Washington for a navicert, stating the character of their shipments and the destination of the goods.[29] The issuance of the navicert did not relieve the vessel of the necessity of stopping at one of the British control ports, but it did cut down the delays previously complained of. In some cases inspectors appointed by the British Consulate supervised the loading and checked the manifest; while the United States cooperated to the extent of urging American shippers to have complete and accurate manifests and of offering to furnish a customs officer to supervise the loading of the cargo and certify to the correctness of the manifest.[30]

INVIOLA-
BILITY
OF POSTAL
CORRE-
SPONDENCE:
*Status of
contraband
sent by
mail*

Does the immunity normally attaching to postal correspondence give protection against the seizure by a belligerent of contraband in the form of bills of exchange, money orders, check, stocks, bonds, and negotiable instruments in general? The question has given rise to acute controversy between neutrals and belligerents, and it would appear as if, here again, the neutrals

[28] See particularly the note of November 7, 1914. Carlton Savage, *op. cit.,* II, 231.

[29] The system is described in detail in Hugh Ritchie, *The "Navicert" System During the World War* (Washington: Carnegie Endowment for International Peace, 1938).

[30] In the Harvard Draft Convention on the Rights and Duties of Neutral States in Naval and Aerial War, the reporter, Professor P. C. Jessup, has worked out an elaborate system of "certificates of neutrality" which the neutral state, in agreement with the belligerents, would issue to its shippers and thereby ensure them against belligerent interference with their trade with other neutrals. See *Am. Journal of Int. Law,* XXXIII (1939), Supplement Section of Documents.

have had to yield for the sake of peace. The United States, as a belligerent in three wars before 1907, had followed the policy of not interfering with mail steamers, except where there was evidence of intent to violate the law in respect to contraband and blockade, and of respecting the public mails of neutral powers when duly certified as such.[31] At the Hague Conference of 1907, in the Convention (XI) Relative to Certain Restrictions with Regard to the Exercise of the Right of Capture in Naval War, it was provided that "the postal correspondence of neutrals or belligerents, whether official or private in character, which may be found on board a neutral or enemy ship at sea, is inviolable" (Art. I). This "inviolability" however, was not to extend to postal correspondence destined for or proceeding from a blockaded port; nor did it exempt neutral mail ships in other respects from the ordinary laws of war applicable to neutral merchant ships; that is, from the obligation to submit to visit and search when that was deemed "absolutely necessary" by the belligerent (as in cases where the cargo of the vessel other than its mailbags might be suspected of containing contraband).[32] The Convention was duly ratified by the United States, as well as by Great Britain.

It was not until January 4, 1916, that the United States found it necessary to complain that the British authorities were removing parcel mail from ships sailing between the United States and neutral European countries. It was agreed, however, that parcel-post articles were in the same class with other merchandise, and the only issue on that point was the illegality of bringing in the ships for search in port. In respect to cor-

Controversy during the World War

[31] The correspondence between the United States and Great Britain during the American Civil War may be found in John Bassett Moore, *A Digest of International Law*, VII, §1201.

[32] The text of the convention may be found in *Treaties, Conventions*, etc., *between the United States and Other Powers*, II, 2348.

respondence proper, the complaint was that by bringing the vessels into port for search the British Government was thereby seeking to justify the censorship of sealed mail on the ground that while in port the vessels and their contents were subject to local regulations, which included censorship of the mails. In reply the British Government, with the French Government joining in the statement, agreed to refrain "on the high seas" from seizing and confiscating genuine "correspondence." This met the issue so far as the *place* of seizure was concerned. But what was meant by genuine "correspondence"?

What is "corre- spondence"?

On May 24 Secretary Lansing gave the case of the United States away. He accepted the statement that genuine correspondence was inviolable, but went on to admit that the belligerents might search "other private sea-borne mails . . . to discover whether they contain articles of enemy ownership carried on belligerent [? neutral] vessels or articles of contraband transmitted under sealed cover as letter mail." The Government of the United States, he said, was "inclined to the opinion" that the class of mail matter which included stocks, bonds, and other securities, money orders, checks and drafts, was to be regarded as of the same nature as merchandise and subject to the same exercise of belligerent rights; whereas correspondence, including shipping documents, money-order lists and similar papers were to be regarded as "genuine correspondence" and "entitled to unmolested passage." [33] For the rest the note dealt with the British practice of forcing vessels to come into port for search where they were deprived of the benefit of the assurances that correspondence would be respected on the high seas.

Search for contraband

But once it was admitted that articles of contraband were not protected by the inviolability of the mails the door was

[33] This important document may be found in Carlton Savage, *op. cit.*, II 498.

wide open. This Secretary Lansing himself saw. The Allies replied to his note on October 12. Five days later, in a private
letter to the President, Secretary Lansing admitted that "as to
the inspection of sealed mail there is a conflict of principles
due to the law of contraband and the theory of inviolability,
principles which are irreconcilable because the superiority of
right of exercise has never been determined." [34] In a memorandum accompanying the letter Mr. Lansing observed that "to
determine whether a mail bag contains contraband articles or
contraband correspondence requires inspection by a belligerent," and that it was manifest that the law of contraband could
not be applied to sealed packets "without their being opened
and inspected." Even in respect to sealed mail destined to neutral countries, the Secretary admitted the doctrine of "ultimate
destination" and observed, "how can the ultimate destination of
sealed mail be determined unless it is opened and inspected." [35]
The belligerents could have asked for nothing more.[36]

The precedents of the World War remained to be quoted   *Treatment*
against the United States in the present war. On January 2,   *of the mails*
1940, the Department of State released to the press its note of   *in the*
protest to Great Britain against the removal by British author- *present war*

[34] *Ibid.*, 528. An interesting sidelight is thrown on the direction of Secretary Lansing's thoughts by his observation in the same note that, in considering the subject he thought "we should bear in mind that, while we are
neutral in the present war, we may be belligerent in the next and may deem
it necessary to do certain things which we now regard extreme restrictions
upon neutrals. It would be unfortunate to tie ourselves too tightly to a proposition which we would regret in the future." It has been well observed that
it is a wise neutral who knows his own future belligerent interests.

[35] *Ibid.*, 529.

[36] Doubtless they had logic on their side and Secretary Lansing saw it,
realizing that a belligerent, with his back to the wall, will press his rights to
the limit. The difficulty for the neutral is to determine where to draw the
line, for each acquiescence in belligerent demands is apt to be followed, as in
this case, by more extreme demands.

ities from British ships and "from American and other neutral
ships" of American mails addressed to neutral countries, and
against the opening and censoring of sealed letter mail sent
from the United States. Specific instances were cited. It was
admitted that Great Britain might censor private mail passing
through the country; but not admitted that the British authorities had the right "to interfere with American mails on American or other neutral ships on the high seas" or the right "to
censor mail on ships which have involuntarily entered British
ports." The eleventh Hague Convention was cited, and the
British practice of taking mails from vessels which "through
some form of duress" were induced to call at designated control
bases was said to be "a clear violation of the immunity provided
by the Hague Convention." [37]

The British Government replied on January 17, insisting that
the immunity conferred by the Hague Convention was "en-
joyed only by genuine postal correspondence," and that a belligerent was therefore at liberty to examine mailbags and, if
necessary, their contents "to assure himself that they constitute such correspondence and not articles of a noxious character such as contraband." The practice of 1914-1918 was cited
as indicating that none of the belligerents accepted the view
that Article I of the Hague Convention "constituted an absolute prohibition of interference with mail bags," and that "the
general right to search for contraband was regarded as covering
a full examination of mails for this purpose." Letter mails, it
was said, might be "used to convey securities, cheques or notes
or again they may be used to send industrial diamonds and
other light contraband." Evidence was given of "an organized
traffic in contraband on a considerable scale between German
sympathisers in the United States and Germany through the
mail." The note concluded with the assertion that it was not

[37] Department of State *Bulletin,* January 6, 1940, p. 3.

believed that the examination of neutral mails was contrary to the obligations of the British Government under international law; but that everything would be done to conduct the examination with as little inconvenience as possible.[38]

A delicate problem is presented by the use of the airplane to carry mails. On January 18, 1940, the British authorities at Bermuda commenced censorship of through-bound mail for Europe carried on the American Clipper. Shortly afterwards it was announced by the Pan American Airways that their planes would thereafter omit the stop at Bermuda and fly direct to the Azores. What now, if the British Government should seek to divert the planes, from their direct course to a neutral port, to a belligerent port, such as Gibraltar, for purposes of a search for contraband which could not be carried out while the plane was in flight? It would seem that neutral planes as such are no more entitled to immunity from search than are neutral vessels, if the belligerent right of search is to be pressed to the limit. Whether the belligerent would not be wise to refrain from pressing his rights too far in this respect is a political rather than a legal question.

[38] Department of State *Bulletin,* January 27, 1940, p. 91. The further British contention, that it was also "in accordance with international law" for belligerents to prevent "intelligence" reaching the enemy "which might assist them in hostile operations," is contrary not only to the letter but to the spirit of the Hague Convention. Such a search into the subject matter of postal correspondence goes far beyond a mere search for contraband.

Airplane mails

VI. NEUTRAL DUTIES

The way of the neutral state is a hard one. It has rights which the belligerents are legally bound to respect, although they do not always do so. But it has also duties of a most burdensome character—duties which one or other of the belligerents is constantly hammering at, lest its enemy profit by their neglect. Some of these duties relate to the enforcement by the neutral state of its rights in respect to the inviolability of its territory. The greater part, however, relate not to resistance against forcible belligerent encroachments but to the maintenance of a delicate balance between the belligerents, known technically as "impartiality," which consists in an elaborate series of rules prescribing just how far the neutral can continue to maintain normal relations with the belligerents without giving them assistance in the conduct of the war.[1]

The duty of the neutral state to enforce respect for the inviolability of its territory has already been discussed indirectly in connection with the enforcement of neutral rights. Here the neutral is sometimes put in a very embarrassing position. It is sovereign within its territory; and as such, it is responsible for

---

[1] Professor Clyde Eagleton justly observes that there is no general "duty of impartiality" imposed upon the neutral state, but only a series of specific duties, apart from which the neutral is free to favor one or other of the belligerents. "Duty of Impartiality on the Part of a Neutral," *Am. Journal of Int. Law,* XXXIV (1939), 99. See, in contrast, Harvard Draft Convention on Neutral Rights and Duties, Art. 4, where the duty of "impartiality" is laid down in somewhat broader terms.

whatever is done within it. But the responsibility may at times exceed the power of the neutral to make it effective. In the famous case of the *General Armstrong,* in which an American brig was attacked by a British squadron in the Portuguese harbor of Fayal in 1814, the Portuguese Governor requested the British commander to refrain from further hostilities after the American ship had temporarily driven off the attacking vessels. But when his request was rejected, the Governor did not attempt to use what forces he had, although admittedly inadequate, to protect the American vessel against renewal of the attack. In consequence the United States pressed a claim for damages on the ground that the neutral was under a duty to enforce its neutrality or pay compensation. The arbitrator, to whom the case was finally submitted, came to the curious conclusion that because the *General Armstrong* had not appealed to the Portuguese Governor before attempting to defend itself the neutral state was released from any further duty than that of pacific intervention.[2]

During the World War Belgium was put in the embarrassing position of either yielding to the demand of Germany that its armies be allowed to cross Belgian neutral and neutralized territory or seeing itself overrun by a more powerful neighbor. It chose to resist and its heroic choice will go down in the annals of history. But could France have brought a claim for compensation if Belgium, knowing of a certainty what was to befall it, had chosen to surrender rather than to fight? Luxemburg, unable to put up any effective resistance whatever, yielded without a struggle; but when the war was over no one thought of holding it to account for its failure to enforce its rights.

Belgium and Luxemburg, 1914

When Great Britain decided late in March that the passage of German ships up and down the long Norwegian coast line

Norway and Denmark, 1940

[2] See John Bassett Moore, *A Digest of International Law,* II, §210; C. G. Fenwick, *Cases on International Law,* p. 750. Above, p. 53.

was in excess of the "right of passage" through neutral territorial waters recognized by international law as within the right of the neutral to concede to belligerents, and proceeded thereupon to lay mines at certain points within the "covered way," the act undoubtedly constituted a violation of the neutrality of Norway. The British Government, through Mr. Churchill, First Lord of the Admiralty, justified the violation on the ground of necessity, and cited the precedent of the World War, in which Great Britain, France, and the United States had gone "together with the Norwegians" to lay mine fields across their territorial waters and across the covered way to prevent the use of the channel by submarines. In any case Norway was obviously in no position to resist.[3] Then, almost simultaneously, came the military invasion of Norway by Germany. Here was more than a mere question of the inviolability of territorial waters. The sovereignty and independence of Norway were now at stake and the Government resisted with all its forces. Denmark, similarly invaded by Germany, surrendered without resistance.[4]

NEUTRAL DUTY OF ABSTENTION

How to keep out of war even when you want to keep out of it is the essential problem of neutral duty. Its difficulty lies partly in the fact that the neutral state must satisfy two opposing belligerents each of whom is keenly watchful to see that

[3] Possibly Norway would not in the first place have permitted its territorial waters to be used by German ships if it had dared risk offending Germany by closing the "covered way." Such is the fate of the small neutral!

[4] The surrender of Denmark raises a difficult problem in respect to the recognition to be given by neutral states to the official acts of the *de jure* Danish government now under duress. Is the government really *de jure* when it is not the free agent it was before the German occupation? Suppose the Danish government, acting under compulsion, ordered all Danish vessels in American ports to transfer control to local German officials; and suppose, further, that the Danish captains refused to obey the orders knowing that they were issued under compulsion. Whose title to the ship would the neutral government protect?

even the slightest neglect on the part of the neutral of its duties may not work to the benefit of the enemy. Here the situation of the weak neutral is one of constant nervous tension, if
by chance its territory is strategically located from the point
of view of belligerent operations. Hence it will go to the extreme limit in seeking to avoid any possible ground of complaint from the belligerents. Let a belligerent plane lose its way
and fly by mistake over neutral Dutch territory, and the Dutch
anti-aircraft guns will risk firing upon it in the solicitude of
the Government to avoid any suggestion of acquiesence even
in an act of no military importance. So well-established is the
tradition of rigorous observance of neutrality that the United
States, although without reason to fear recriminations by the
belligerents, has equalled the weak neutral in its solicitude to
maintain a technically legal position in spite of strong sympathy at times with one or other of the belligerents.

But the more fundamental difficulty is due to the fact that *Practical*
war does not completely cut off belligerents from neutrals. If *problems it*
upon the outbreak of war an impassable barrier, moral as well *presents*
as material, were immediately to be erected around the neutral
state, the problem of neutral duty would be a simple one. Such,
however, is not the way the law has developed; and the law has
obviously reflected social and economic conditions. What the
law has prescribed is that the neutral state as a state must not
take sides in the war. But that does not mean that it must cut
itself off from all contacts with the belligerents; and the fact
that certain of these contacts involve some degree of indirect
assistance to one of the belligerents more than to the other of
fers at times a fertile field for controversy. Again, when the law
says that a neutral state must not take sides that does not
mean that the individual citizens of the state may not take
sides; and the problem is to determine how far the government
of the neutral state must restrain them in order to avoid the

imputation that their acts as individuals are compromising the neutral position of the state itself. We have, therefore, three practical problems: what duties are exacted of the government of the neutral state in respect to its own official conduct; what contacts may it permit belligerents to maintain with its territory; and what restraints must the neutral government impose upon the conduct of its citizens? Needless to say we shall not expect logic or consistency in the rules of international law that have been developed to meet these problems. For they are rules that are the result for the most part of usages and customs which of their nature have been slow to respond to changing conditions; while such international conventions as can be said to have legal value have for the most part been formulated in such general terms as to offer only an inadequate solution for the specific issues that actual war has presented.

Official state conduct The rule is now established that the neutral state, in so far as it is represented by the official acts of its government, must refrain from giving any direct assistance to either belligerent in the prosecution of the war. The law has changed since 1793 when Secretary Jefferson, justifying himself no doubt by Vattel's treatise,[5] could hold that it was "an essential character of neutrality, to furnish no aids (not stipulated by treaty), to one party which we are not equally ready to furnish to the other." [6] Jefferson found his hands tied, unfortunately, by the treaty of 1778 with France; but he did his best to interpret it in such a way as to be consistent with neutrality. At the Hague Conference of 1907 it was stated in clear and definite terms that "the supply, in any manner, directly or indirectly, by a neutral Power to a belligerent Power, of war-ships, ammunition, or war

[5] See above, p. 11.

[6] Thomas Jefferson to T. Pinckney (Minister to Great Britain), September 7, 1793. Carlton Savage, *op. cit.*, I, 166.

material of any kind whatever is forbidden."[7] Prior treaty
obligations would now be no ground for discrimination.

Queries may be raised on a few specific items in this connection. As early as 1798 the United States refused to make a loan
of money to France on ground that it would be a violation of
neutrality.[8] This is clearly the law today; but would it cover
the case of a loan, or credits, for the purchase of surplus commodities not falling within the class of "war material" to which
the Hague Convention refers? The loan made to Finland by the
Export-Import Bank while hostilities with Russia were in progress may be defended on the ground that Russia and Finland
were not technically "at war."[9] Could it also be defended on
the ground that the use of the funds was limited to the purchase of the particular commodities for the sale of which the
Export-Import Bank was created? Doubtless not, but the case
is not clear. In 1914 the United States interpreted its neutral
duty as preventing a "sale" by the Government itself to a belligerent nation, apart from the innocent character of the goods
sold.[10] This was doubtless going beyond the letter of the law.
The Harvard Draft Convention on Neutrality raises the question whether the Government of the United States, which has
a monopoly of the production and sale of helium, could license
the sale of it to a belligerent; and, in the Comment, expresses
the opinion that the export of a quantity great enough to be of
military importance would be in violation of neutral duty.[11]
Whether the sale by a neutral government of nonmilitary goods
made in state-owned factories would be in violation of neutral

[7] Convention (XIII) Concerning the Rights and Duties of Neutral Powers in Naval War, Art. 6.

[8] John Bassett Moore, *A Digest of International Law*, VII, §1312.

[9] See below, p. 146.

[10] Francis Deák and Philip C. Jessup, *A Collection of Neutrality Laws of
Various Countries*, II, 1256.

[11] *Am. Journal of Int. Law*, XXXIII (1939), Supp., 242.

Official
expressions
of opinion

duty is an open question. It is but one of the many problems due to the fact that totalitarian governments have taken over so many of the commercial activities formerly engaged in by private persons.[12]

What of expressions of opinion by public officers favorable or unfavorable to the cause of one or other of the belligerents? Here the law is in process of change, and it is impossible to lay down a rigid rule. As far back as 1816 Secretary of State Monroe refused to apologize for remarks of the postmaster at Baltimore reflecting upon the French Government. Mr. Monroe was doubtless wrong in this case in saying that the Government could exercise no control in such cases, for there is a clear distinction between acts of public officials, however minor, and acts of individual citizens.[13] In 1914, while President Wilson went further than was necessary in his appeal of August 18 to the American people to be "impartial in thought as well as in action," there is no doubt that the Government of the United States recognized a duty on the part of officers of the neutral state to refrain from any statement that might be interpreted as approval of the cause of one of the belligerents or condemnation of that of the other.

But by 1939 conditions had changed. The many efforts made to prevent war by condemning acts of aggression and planning discriminatory economic policies towards aggressors had made governments more outspoken. While the Proclamation of Neutrality of September 5 stated that the United States was "on terms of friendship and amity with the contending powers," and the President's radio address two days earlier strictly refrained from taking sides, by the time Congress was called in special session on September 21 the President felt at liberty to use strong phrases about "acts of aggression," the trend toward

[12] See below, p. 140.
[13] See, on this point, C. G. Fenwick, *International Law* (1934), pp. 210 ff.

"further acts of military conquest," "forces which assault the foundations of civilization,"—all of which were as clearly directed against the Government of Germany as if it had been specifically mentioned. More recently in the presence of the invasion of Norway and Denmark by Germany, the President issued a statement on April 13 declaring that "force and military aggression are once more on the march against small nations" and expressing the strong "disapprobation of such unlawful exercise of force." By this time it was clear that the "friendship and amity" of the neutrality proclamation of September 5 was a purely perfunctory attitude.

What contacts may the neutral state maintain with the belligerents of a semi-official character even though they involve some degree of indirect assistance to the belligerents, and possibly more to one than to the other? They consist chiefly in certain courtesies which the neutral state may show, or better, privileges which it may grant, to belligerent public and private ships in its ports. These privileges had their origin back in the days of sailing vessels, when the distinction between a warship and a merchant ship was not clearly marked, and when wars were too frequent and too informal in character to raise any question of the duty of the neutral to accord any different treatment to a foreign warship in time of war from that accorded in time of peace. Special treaties were frequently concluded stipulating the privileges which the contracting parties would give to each others' public vessels in time of war. The treaty between the United States and France in 1778, for example, provided that it should be lawful for the ships of war of either party to bring their prizes into the ports of the other, and that no shelter should be given to vessels bringing prizes taken from the subjects of the contracting parties.[14] When

[14] Francis Deák and Philip C. Jessup, eds., *A Collection of Neutrality Laws, Regulations and Treaties of Various Countries*, II, 1317.

these special treaty privileges became no longer consistent with neutrality, neutral states began to draw up regulations applicable equally to both of the belligerents. Codification was attempted at the Hague Conference of 1907, and the rules there laid down disposed of most of the controversial points.

Specific rules
It is now generally accepted that twenty-four hours is the maximum period of stay in port to be permitted to belligerent warships. The Hague Convention of 1907 fixed that period in default of special provisions to the contrary in the laws of the neutral power, thus making it easier for the small neutral to enforce the rule. The United States followed the twenty-four-hour rule in 1914 and is following it in the present war. So also are most, if not all, of the American Republics.

The earlier practice of permitting belligerent warships and privateers to make repairs in neutral ports has now been strictly limited. The United States took the lead in 1793 in holding that belligerents must not be allowed "to increase their force" within the ports of the United States.[15] The Hague Convention of 1907 specified that the repairs must be only such as were absolutely necessary to render the warship seaworthy and must not add in any manner whatsoever to its fighting force. This is now the general rule. When the *Graf Spee* took refuge in the harbor of Montevideo on December 13, 1939, the German commander requested the Uruguayan Government to allow him to remain an indefinite period in order to make necessary repairs. The Uruguayan Government examined the vessel to determine the extent of repairs necessary to make it seaworthy and ordered it to make the repairs and leave port in seventy-two hours. The vessel left, but unfortunately did not go very far.[16]

It should be noted that the limited privileges granted to bel-

[15] The following year, 1794, it was made a penal offense for individuals to cooperate in furnishing such repairs to belligerent warships. See below, p. 116.

[16] Other aspects of the *Graf Spee* case are discussed above, p. 58.

ligerent warships in neutral ports are privileges only, not rights. At any time the neutral state is free to deny such privileges altogether, or to restrict them further than the degree required by international conventions. There can be no question of the right of the United States to exclude submarines from its ports and territorial waters, as has been done by executive degree in pursuance of the terms of the neutrality act of 1939.[17] The United States might also, if it chose to do so, regard armed merchant ships as in the class of warships, and limit their privileges in port accordingly. This, however, has not yet been done by executive decree, although the act of 1939 empowers the President to make proclamation excluding them whenever he believes it to be necessary to the peace and safety of the United States.

May a neutral state permit a belligerent to bring into its neutral ports a prize of war of enemy or of neutral nationality? The problem is an old one, due to the numerous privateers which in former times roamed the seas in search of prey and often sought to sell their prizes in the nearest neutral port in order to sally forth and make another capture. Treaties were entered into, as we have seen in the case of the United States and France, providing for the admission of prizes captured by the contracting parties. With the disappearance of privateering and of special favors, the question was considered at the Hague Conference of 1907 and the conclusion was reached, in the Convention Concerning the Rights and Duties of Neutral Powers in Naval War, that prizes might be brought into a neutral port by a belligerent on account of unseaworthiness, stress of weather, or want of fuel or provisions. If brought into port under any other circumstances the prize must be released by the neutral state. In the well-known case of the *Appam*, which

Prizes brought into neutral ports

[17] See above, p. 56.

involved a British merchant vessel captured by a German cruiser and brought into the port of Norfolk to be interned, the Supreme Court of the United States held that the effort "to make of an American port a depository of captured vessels with a view to keeping them there indefinitely" was a breach of neutrality as tested by the traditional policy of the United States and by the Hague Convention Concerning the Rights and Duties of Neutral Powers.

Case of the "City of Flint"

On October 9, 1939, the American vessel, *City of Flint,* with a mixed cargo destined to British ports, was captured by a German warship on the high seas on ground of carriage of contraband. A prize crew was put on board, and the vessel, after touching at a Norwegian port and being ordered to depart, was brought into the harbor of Murmansk, Russia, on October 23, because of alleged "sea damage." The Soviet authorities at first interned the German prize crew, apparently ignoring the claim that the inability of the vessel to proceed for want of navigation charts constituted "damage" or "unseaworthiness." Subsequently the prize crew was released on the ground that the reason for entering Murmansk was defective machinery which required repairs. The United States insisted that, in view of the absence of any "justifiable grounds such as are prescribed by international law" for taking the vessel into a neutral port, the vessel should be turned over to the American crew. This was refused by the Soviet authorities, but the vessel was ordered to leave port, still being in charge of its German prize crew. On its way down the Norwegian coast the vessel stopped at Haugesund to deliver one of the American sailors, who was ill, to the American consul. The Norwegian naval authorities investigated the situation but did not find the seaman sufficiently ill to justify permitting the vessel to anchor. Nevertheless the vessel did anchor; whereupon the Norwegian authori-

ties interned the German prize crew and released the vessel to
its American crew.[18]

Just as it is the duty of the neutral state to intern persons
belonging to the armed forces of the belligerents in case they
should come within its territory, so also is it its duty to intern
the officers and crew of a belligerent warship both when the
vessel itself seeks asylum in the neutral port or when the officers and crew, having lost their vessel at sea, come as shipwrecked persons to the shelter of the neutral port. In the case
of the *Graf Spee,* which met with shipwreck by its own act,
the officers and crew asked the Argentine Government to set
them at liberty on the ground that they arrived at their destination, not as shipwrecked sailors but as passengers on board
Argentine neutral craft. The Argentine Government, however,
looked behind the subterfuge and ordered internment.[19]

In order to scuttle his vessel without danger to his crew the
captain of the *Graf Spee* arranged that the German merchant
ship *Tacoma* should accompany the vessel to its appointed
place of suicide and take on board the officers and crew of the
doomed vessel. This the *Tacoma* did. After the officers and
crew had been retransferred to smaller Argentine craft the *Tacoma* returned to Montevideo, where it was promptly interned,
together with its officers and crew, by the Uruguayan Government. The ground of internment was the unneutral act of the

---

[18] Department of State *Bulletin,* October 28, 1939, p. 429; November 4,
p. 457.

[19] The Argentine Government, in a decree of December 19, 1939, taking
note of the fact that the Hague Convention of 1899 for the Adaptation to
Maritime Warfare of the Principles of the Geneva Convention of 1864 provided that sick, wounded, and shipwrecked persons arriving in neutral territory from belligerent warships should be guarded by the neutral state, and
citing similar action by the Argentine Government during the World War,
interned the commander and officers in the city of Buenos Aires and the
crew in one of the provinces of the interior. See Pan American Union, *Law
and Treaty Series,* No. 13, p. 6.

Tacoma in giving assistance to a belligerent warship. The fact that the captain of the *Tacoma* had put himself under orders of the commander of the *Graf Spee* was sufficient to constitute the *Tacoma* an auxiliary warship.[20]

Belligerent passage through neutral territorial waters

Has the neutral state a duty to prevent the passage of belligerent warships through its territorial waters? Except for the recent crisis in Norway there would scarcely have been need to put the question, since the general principle, as stated by the Hague Convention Concerning the Rights and Duties of Neutral Powers that "the neutrality of a Power is not affected by the mere passage through its territorial waters of warships or prizes belonging to belligerents," met with no opposition at the Conference. The difference of opinion, such as there was, centered about the *right* of the neutral to prohibit the passage rather than its duty to do so. The "passage" referred to in the Hague Convention was obviously "innocent passage." Did that cover the use of the long coast line of Norway by German warships as a base of naval operation from which attacks could be made upon merchant vessels trading between Norway and Great Britain, or its use by German merchant vessels as a means of escape from capture by British warships? The rule of "innocent passage" is too vague to afford an answer. At any rate Great Britain came to the conclusion at the time of the *Altmark* affair that the Norwegian Government should not permit the kind of use that the Germans were making of its territorial waters;[21] with results that are unhappily only too well known.

RESTRAINTS UPON INDIVIDUAL PERSONS

As a practical matter by far the heaviest duties of a neutral state consist in the restraints which they find it necessary to

[20] The facts and the justification for the action taken by the Uruguayan Government in both the *Graf Spee* and the *Tacoma* cases are set forth in detail in the Uruguayan Blue Book, issued shortly after the events.

[21] See above, pp. 53, 103.

put upon their citizens and other persons within their jurisdiction to prevent them from giving certain forms of aid to the
belligerents, which by international law have come to be held
as compromising the neutrality of the state. If we take the year
1794, the date of the first neutrality legislation of the United
States, as the beginning of the development of the modern
law of neutral duties in this connection, custom and convention have combined to draw a line between acts of individuals
which would amount to direct and immediate military aid to
the belligerents and acts which are of less direct and immediate aid. The former it is the duty of the neutral to prevent.
The latter, although they may be of far more substantial aid to
the belligerents, the neutral is not bound to prevent. There is
no logic in the situation, except the logic of adjusting laws to
the practical situations which the neutral state is called upon
to meet.

In pursuance of the duty of the United States as a neutral   *Neutrality*
to prevent individuals within its jurisdiction from performing   *acts*
the various acts regarded as coming within the forbidden class,
Congress has passed a number of "neutrality acts" defining in
detail the prohibited offenses against neutrality and prescribing penalties for their commission. These acts are purely domestic legislation, enacted, indeed, to fulfill what have been
believed to be the neutral duties of the United States under
international law, but not necessarily coinciding with the rules
of international law on the subject. In fact the neutrality legislation of the United States has on the whole been stricter in
its prohibitions than the international law of neutrality has
required.[22]

[22] It is important to distinguish these "neutrality acts," passed in order
to enable the Government of the United States to meet its obligations under
international law, from the so-called "neutrality" legislation enacted since
1935, the purpose of which has been not the fulfillment of the duties of the

Specific
offenses

All Americans are familiar with the story of the landing of Citizen Genêt at Charleston in 1793 and of his undue zeal in distributing commissions for the fitting out of French privateers in that port. The lure of privateering was a strong one in those days, for the profits from the sale of prizes were large and the risks involved in their capture were such as sailors were accustomed to. Accepting these foreign commissions, Americans proceeded to fit out and arm their vessels in the ports of the United States, with intent to capture British vessels in aid of the French cause, but to their own gain as well. In addition, enlistments of American citizens in the cause of France were going on freely; while strong sympathy for the French revolutionary cause and a desire to seize the opportunity to capture New Orleans, then in the possession of Spain, and possibly the Floridas, led to the formation of military expeditions in Kentucky which the Governor of the State refused to prevent. President Washington had, in his proclamation of neutrality on April 22, warned that offenders "under the law of nations" would be prosecuted; but something more was needed if the offenders were to be convicted. In consequence, the President, in his annual address in December, called upon Congress to "extend the legal code." Congress responded, and on June 5, 1794, passed an act which set a standard of neutral conduct that was destined to have a marked effect upon the development of the international law of neutral duty. The act prohibited, within the territory or jurisdiction of the United States, the acceptance and exercise of a commission to serve a foreign prince or state, the enlistment or hiring to enlist in the service of a belligerent, the hiring to enlist abroad, the fitting out and

United States as a neutral but the prohibition to American citizens of certain commercial and personal contacts with the belligerents which, however lawful at international law, might tend to influence public opinion to be favorable to one side or hostile to the other. See above, p. 44.

arming within the ports of the United States of vessels intended to be used in the service of a foreign state against another foreign state with which the United States was at peace, augmenting the force of any ship of war of a belligerent, and setting on foot a military expedition against the territory of a belligerent state with which the United States was at peace.[23] These offenses still form the chief provisions of our present neutrality legislation.[24]

Sales of merchant ships

The wars of the South American provinces to secure their independence created new problems of neutrality, and in 1818 the provisions of the act of 1794 were extended to apply to colonies and districts which could not technically be brought under the head of "foreign prince or state." At this time an effort was made in Congress to prohibit the sale to a belligerent of an armed vessel built and equipped in a port of the United States. The effort failed; and five years later, in 1822, the Supreme Court held, in the case of the *Santissima Trinidad*,[25] that the sending of an armed vessel to a foreign port for sale was to be regarded as no more than the sale of so much contraband, a commercial venture exposing the persons engaged in it to the penalty of capture and confiscation of the ship, but not otherwise unlawful. The court was referring to a sale in a foreign port. What of a sale of such a vessel in a neutral port; what of building a vessel of war in a neutral port to the order of a belligerent, even though the armament of the vessel be added in another neutral port?

Case of the "Alabama"

The story of the *Alabama* is a classic in the history of the

[23] Francis Deák and Philip C. Jessup, *op. cit.*, II, 1079.

[24] They were reenacted, with additions, in the Revised Statutes of 1874, and again reenacted in the "Penal Code of the United States" of March 4, 1909. They were incorporated in Title 18, Secs. 21-30, of the United States Code of 1934.

[25] 7 Wheaton 283 (1822). C. G. Fenwick, *Cases on International Law*, p. 752.

118   foreign relations of the United States.[26] The claim brought by
the United States against Great Britain for damages for the
losses incurred by the depredations of the vessel in the service
of the Confederate States was arbitrated at Geneva under the
rules set forth in the treaty of Washington. Scholars have de-
bated at length whether the provision of the treaty, that a neutral state was bound "to use due diligence" to prevent the
fitting out, arming, or equipping within its jurisdiction of any
vessel which it had reasonable ground to believe was intended
to carry on war against a power with which it was at peace,
was a rule of international law at the time the *Alabama* left
the British port. At any rate the rule was adopted in substance
at the Hague Conference of 1907, with the change, however,
that the somewhat uncertain phrase "due diligence" was replaced by the phrase "a neutral government is bound to em-
ploy the means at its disposal" to prevent the acts in question.

During the World War, while the United States was still a
neutral, it was found necessary to supplement existing legislation by a number of new provisions. A joint resolution of
March 4, 1915, sought to prevent the territorial waters of the
United States from being made a "base of operations" for the
armed forces of the belligerents, by providing that the collec-
tors of customs might withhold clearance from vessels believed
to be about to carry fuel, arms, ammunition, men, or supplies
to any warship or supply ship of a belligerent nation. This law
was strengthened by the act of June 15, 1917, which contained
a further provision directed against the building, arming, or
equipping of a vessel of war with intent that it should be delivered to a belligerent or with reasonable cause to believe that
it would be employed in the service of a belligerent after its

[26] For details of the case, see Samuel F. Bemis, *A Diplomatic History of
the United States*, pp. 337 ff.; C. G. Fenwick, *Cases on International Law*,
p. 639.

departure from the jurisdiction of the United States. Thus was
the doctrine of the *Alabama* case implemented, even if the
Hague Convention of 1907 was not technically binding.

During the present war the neutral American states have *"Auxiliary*
found it all the more necessary to prevent their waters from *transports"*
being made a base of operations by the belligerents in order to
avoid any criticism that the "security zone" established by the
Declaration of Panama might be serving as a refuge or sanctuary for one belligerent or the other. If merchant vessels
should be permitted to leave neutral ports and make contacts
with belligerent warships within the zone, not only would there
be a question of neglect of neutral duty under international
law, but valid objections would be raised against the claim of
the neutral American states that the security zone should remain free from hostilities. In consequence, the Inter-American
Neutrality Committee, acting in response to an inquiry from
the Government of Uruguay arising out of the *Tacoma* case,
drew up under date of February 2, 1940, a Recommendation
on Vessels used as Auxiliary Transports, which contains a series
of suggested rules for preventing as far as possible any such
contacts.[27]

In spite of the strict provisions of neutrality laws of the *Airplanes*
United States in respect to the fitting out and arming of ves- *as contra-*
sels in the ports of the United States with intent that they shall *band*
be used in the service of a belligerent, airplanes are not regarded as in the class of vessels of war even when built for war
purposes, and they may be sold and exported upon the same
footing with other contraband of war. During the World War
the German Government protested against the delivery of
American-built hydroplanes to the Allies; but the Department
of State replied that the fact that such planes were "fitted with
apparatus to rise from and alight upon the sea" did not give

[27] See Pan American Union, *Law and Treaty Series,* No. 13, p. 61.

them the character of "vessels" so as to bring them within the rules of international law applicable to such.[28] In view, however, of the development of planes specially built for combat purposes, the Hague Air Rules of 1923 provided that the neutral state must prevent the departure from its jurisdiction "of an aircraft in a condition to make a hostile attack against a belligerent power." [29] This provision, however, even had it been ratified, would have required little more than the present practice of delivering American planes by pushing them over the Canadian border.[30]

PERMIS-
SIBLE
ACTS OF
CITIZENS

A wide field for controversy arises when we turn from the acts of individuals within its jurisdiction which it is agreed that the neutral state is under obligation to prevent to the acts which it need not prevent. For not only is there little logic in the distinction between the two sets of acts on the basis of the direct or less direct military aid which they give to the belligerent; but there is even less logic in the distinction between acts which the state may not perform in its corporate capacity

[28] *American White Book,* II, 145.

[29] For the text of the draft code, see *Am. Journal of Int. Law,* XVII (1923), Supp., 242; and John Bassett Moore, *International Law and Some Current Illusions,* p. 210 ff.

[30] It would seem just as well that Germany is not in a position to protest effectively against the sale of American bombing planes to the Allies; or better, it would seem desirable that Germany should not be in such a position. For it is difficult to reconcile their sale with the doctrines advanced by the United States in the *Alabama* case. Here, again, it would seem that the American people have compromised with neutrality, not really having any faith in it, or any love for it, under the conditions of the present war. The Harvard Draft Convention on the Rights and Duties of Neutral States goes the whole length in forbidding (Article 99) not only the fitting out and arming of aircraft but the flight from neutral territory of aircraft intended to engage in hostile operations or to perform services of a military character for a belligerent. But the Draft was the work of technicians, who could not take into account the fact that the American people might want to be neutral, but not too neutral.

as a state and acts which individual citizens of the state may be allowed to undertake upon their own initiative. Here, as in other parts of the law, logic has had to yield to expediency; and to make the situation worse, conditions have kept continually changing.

It is the traditional rule that neutral states are not under a duty to prevent expressions of opinion by their citizens through press and platform and now through radio broadcasting, no matter how hostile these may be to one or other of the belligerents. President Wilson's appeal to the American people in 1914 to be "impartial in thought as well as in action" and to put a curb upon their "sentiments" as well as upon transactions "that might be construed as a preference of one party to the struggle before another" had no basis whatever in international law, whatever its merits as a matter of domestic policy. To suppress freedom of speech in the interests of neutrality is a step that no democratic government would consider taking. It seems, however, that modern totalitarian governments take another view of the matter.[31]

Expressions of opinion

While the neutral state may not itself make loans to the belligerents, it is not called upon to prevent its individual citizens from making them. In August, 1914, the Department of State sought to discourage loans by American bankers to the bellig-

Loans of money

---

[31] On February 29, 1940, Dr. Goebbels, Reich Propaganda Minister, was reported as having stated in a public address that Germany could not put up with a definition of neutrality which referred only to military and not to political neutrality. "We cannot," he said, "allow an obvious difference between the neutrality of a State and the neutrality of its public opinion. It is not sufficient that the Government should declare its neutrality in this war while public opinion in the same State is free to abuse as much as it wishes." He then asserted that while Germany had "by no means any intention to suppress the freedom of opinion in neutral States," yet that freedom "must not be misused to insult systematically belligerent Powers." How such misuse could be prevented except by suppressing freedom of speech he did not stop to explain.

erents as being "inconsistent with the true spirit of neutrality." But the effort met with no success; and it was not long before loans, chiefly in the form of credits for the purchase of supplies, were being freely made. After the war was over, as we have seen, it came to be believed by many persons that the loans made to the Allies were in part the basis of the propaganda that had led to the entrance of the United States into the war; with the result that the act of February 29, 1936, made it unlawful, with certain exceptions, for any person in the United States "to purchase, sell or exchange bonds, securities or other obligations of a belligerent" or "to make any loan or extend any credit" to a belligerent.[32] To make assurance doubly sure, by the act of May 1, 1937, even "contributions" were forbidden.[33]

Sale of munitions of war

The difficult problem is that presented by the sale of munitions of war. In 1793 Secretary Jefferson, in reply to complaints from Great Britain, laid down the rule which formed the policy of the United States down to the year 1935. "We have answered," he said, "that our citizens have always been free to make, vend, and export arms; that it is the constant occupation and livelihood of some of them. To suppress their callings, the only means, perhaps, of their subsistence, because a war exists in foreign and distant countries, in which we have no concern, would scarcely be expected. It would be hard in principle and impossible in practice. The law of nations, therefore, respecting the rights of those at peace, has not required from them such an internal derangement in their occupations. It is satisfied with the external penalty pronounced in the Presi-

[32] See above, p. 38.

[33] It would seem that a man who has made a contribution is already pretty well committed to the side to which he has made his contribution. But Congress in 1937 was possessed of the idea that sentiments and money go very close in hand.

dent's proclamation, that of confiscation of such portion of these arms as shall fall into the hands of any of the belligerent Powers on their way to the ports of their enemies."[34]

The limitations in Jefferson's statement were clear enough. But as time went on his principle was reasserted by succeeding Secretaries of State in broader form.[35] At the Hague Conference of 1907 the Convention (V) Respecting the Rights and Duties of Neutral Powers and Persons in War on Land laid down the broad rule that "a neutral power is not called upon to prevent the export or transport, on behalf of one or other of the belligerents, of arms, munitions of war, or, in general, of anything which can be of use to an army or a fleet." It remained, however, for the World War to show how the Hague Conference had evaded the real issue. For the situation was now presented in which one of the opposing belligerent groups drew heavily upon the United States, while the other was, by reason of the superior navy of the enemy, almost entirely cut off from them. That might have been passed by as part of the fortunes of war had it not been for the fact that the trade in arms soon exceeded the capacity of existing munitions factories and new factories were built to meet the demand. On April 4, 1915, Germany urged that if the people of the United States wanted to observe "a true neutrality" they would stop the "one-sided supply" or at least make use of it to force Great Britain to desist from unlawful interference with neutral trade.[36] In reply Secretary Bryan took the position that "any change in its [this Government's] own laws of neutrality during the progress of a war which would affect unequally the relations of the United States with the nations at war would be an unjustifiable de-

World War developments

[34] *American State Papers, Foreign Relations,* I, 147.
[35] See John Bassett Moore, *A Digest of International Law,* VII, §1308.
[36] *American White Book,* I, 73.

124   parture from the principle of strict neutrality." [37] Some months later the Austro-Hungarian Government pointed out that the arms industry had "soared to unimagined heights," and that the law should be changed to meet changing conditions. In his reply on August 12 to the Austro-Hungarian complaint, Secretary Lansing denied that Government's "assertion of an obligation to change or modify the rules of international usage." He then went on to argue that there was a "practical and substantial reason for not prohibiting trade in military supplies," namely, that an advantage would lie with the nation better prepared for war and in consequence states would be tempted to accumulate in time of peace vast stores of arms; so that the principle of prohibiting sales of arms to belligerents "would force militarism on the world." [38]

It is difficult to justify the position taken by Secretary Lansing when he went to the length of implying that the United States could not, consistently with the rules of international law, so much as restrict the trade in arms to the normal pre-war productive capacity of American factories.[39] But the main body of his argument was sound, that a neutral cannot be called upon to "equalize" conditions as between the belligerents, and to deny to one side goods which they are able to buy in order to offset the inability of the other to obtain access to the goods.

Recent legisla- tion   When, in the year 1935, the United States decided to change its policy in respect to the shipment of arms to belligerents in time of war, it did so not because of the recognition of any in-

[37] Carlton Savage, *op. cit.*, II, 297.

[38] Carlton Savage, *op. cit.*, II, 368.

[39] The Secretary's argument against changes in the rules of international law in time of war must be read in the light of his qualification that changes are only permissible when made by the neutral power "in order to protect its own rights. The right and the duty to determine when this necessity exists rests with the neutral, not with the belligerent." See above, p. 45.

ternational duty to do so, but simply because of certain national interests which it believed would be promoted by such
legislation.[40] When, four years later, Congress and the President came to the conclusion that the interests of the country
would be better served by lifting the absolute embargo on arms
and substituting for it a system of sales on the "cash and carry"
plan, it cannot be maintained that as a matter of international
law the belligerent who had profited by the embargo had acquired a vested right in its continuance. The United States had
a legal right to do what every other neutral state was free to
do, and neither of the belligerents had any legal justification
for inquiring into the variety of motives that led to the change
of policy.[41]

[40] See above, p. 34.
[41] See above, p. 46.

VII. SPECIAL PROBLEMS OF THE
PRESENT WAR

NEUTRAL
SOLIDAR-
ITY IN
AMERICA

The idea that in the event of war the American Republics were to endeavor "to adopt in their character as neutrals a common and solidary attitude" goes back, as we have seen, to the Argentine Anti-War Treaty of 1933.[1] At that time the object of seeking a unified policy of neutrality was as a means for the maintenance of peace by shortening the duration of a possible conflict or by deterring in advance the commission of acts of aggression. In like manner the agreement reached by the American Republics at Buenos Aires in 1936 contemplated a unified policy of neutrality "in order to discourage or prevent the spread or prolongation of hostilities," this time the effort being limited to the case of hostilities between two or more of the American Republics themselves.[2] In neither case was there a suggestion of a common attitude of neutrality as a means of protecting the American Republics as a body against the effects of a war in another part of the world.

But if the pledges relating to a common neutrality policy did not anticipate the dangers from a general war in Europe the provisions of other inter-American treaties clearly did so. In 1936, at Buenos Aires, the Convention for the Maintenance, Preservation, and Re-establishment of Peace [3] provided (Article 1) that "in the event that the peace of the American Re-

[1] See above, p. 21.
[2] See above, p. 21.
[3] For the text of the convention, see Pan American Union, *Congress and Conference Series,* No. 22, p. 33.

publics is menaced" there should be consultation "for the purpose of finding and adopting methods of peaceful cooperation"; and it was further provided (Article 2) that, in addition to the case of a war between American states, "in the event of an international war outside America which might menace the peace of the American Republics, such consultation shall also take place to determine the proper time and manner in which the signatory States, if they so desire, may eventually cooperate in some action tending to preserve the peace of the American Continent." This broad agreement to consult in the presence of danger from "outside America" was reaffirmed in the Declaration of Lima, adopted at the Eighth International Conference of American States, held at Lima, 1938, in which, following a reaffirmation of "continental solidarity," provision was made for machinery of cooperation by means of a meeting of the Foreign Ministers of the American states or of their specially designated representatives.[4]

Upon the outbreak of war in Europe it was apparent that a situation had arisen such as had been contemplated by the Buenos Aires Convention and the Lima Declaration, justifying the initiation of the procedure of consultation. The Government of Panamá extended invitations for a meeting at Panamá; and on September 23 the meeting convened, thirteen governments being represented by their ministers of foreign affairs and eight by representatives of the ministers. The meeting devoted itself primarily to problems of neutrality, although other political problems were on the agenda and important steps were taken to meet economic problems arising out of the European conflict.[5]

The Meeting at Panamá

[4] For the text of the agreement see Pan American Union, *Congress and Conference Series*, No. 27, p. 92.

[5] For the texts of the declarations and resolutions adopted by the Panamá Meeting, see Pan American Union, *Congress and Conference Series*, No. 29.

In its General Declaration of Neutrality of the American
Republics the Meeting of Foreign Ministers at Panamá recognized the need of "common and solidary attitudes" with reference to the possible threat to the security of the American
Republics from the European war, and, after affirming the
"unanimous intention" of the American Republics "not to become involved in the European conflict" the meeting declared
that it was desirable to state the "standards of conduct" which
the American Republics proposed to follow "in order to maintain their status as neutral states and fulfill their neutral duties,
as well as require the recognition of the rights inherent in such
a status." The Meeting then undertook to set forth the "standards" of neutral conduct which the American Republics proposed to observe, reciting in detail certain rules of international
law to be followed in relation to the belligerents. In the closing
paragraph of the Declaration the Meeting provided that "with
a view to studying and formulating recommendations with
respect to the problems of neutrality, in the light of experience
and changing circumstances" there should be established, for
the duration of the European war, an Inter-American Neutrality Committee, composed of seven experts in international
law, who were to be designated by the Governing Board of the
Pan American Union.

The Inter-American Neutrality Committee held its first
meeting at Rio de Janeiro on January 15, 1940.[6] Before it were

[6] At its opening meeting the Committee consisted of the following mem-
bers: Luiz A. Podestá Costa, of Argentina; Afranio de Mello Franco, of
Brazil; Mariano Fontecilla, of Chile; Alejandro de Aguilar Machado, of
Costa Rica; Charles G. Fenwick, of the United States; Roberto Córdova, of
Mexico; and Gustavo Herrera, of Venezuela. Señor Aguilar Machado was
replaced in March by Manuel F. Jimenez. It is important to observe that
the individual members of the Committee owe their appointments to the
Governing Board of the Pan American Union and act, not as representatives
of the particular states of which they are nationals, but as representatives of

requests from a number of American governments for recommendations on specific problems of neutrality which concerned them. The Government of Uruguay in particular was concerned with situations arising out of the scuttling of the *Graf Spee* outside of the harbor of Montevideo and the assistance rendered to the pocket battleship in that act by the steamship *Tacoma*. The Committee, therefore, proceeded to formulate regulations in respect to the specific topics of internment, submarines, and auxiliary transports.[7]

Most significant of the agreements reached at the Panamá meeting was doubtless the Declaration of Panamá which established a "zone of security" around the American continent, to be kept free of belligerent operations.[8] Here was a question not of following established rules of international law but of creating a new rule. The preamble of the Declaration called attention to the unusual character of the war in its effects upon the fundamental interests of America and to the absence of any justification that the interests of the belligerents should prevail over the rights of neutrals; there was nothing in the nature of the war to justify any obstruction to inter-American communications which, important as they were, called for adequate protection. For these reasons the Governments of the American Republics declared that "as a measure of continental self-protection" they were "as of inherent right" entitled to have the waters adjacent to the American continent "free from the commission of any hostile act" by any non-American belligerent nation. Then followed a demarcation of the proposed

The Declaration of Panamá: the "security zone"

---

the American states as a whole. The recommendations of the Committee are transmitted, through the Pan American Union, to the Governments of the American Republics. The Committee is thus a unique expression of Pan American solidarity.

[7] For the texts of recommendations of the committee, see Pan American Union, *Law and Treaty Series,* No. 13.

[8] For the text, see Appendix C.

"zone of security," which began at the terminus of the United States-Canada boundary in Passamaquoddy Bay and followed east, south, west, and north to the Pacific terminus of the United States-Canada boundary in the Strait of Juan de Fuca.

It was agreed in the Declaration that the American Republics would endeavor, "through joint representation" to the belligerents "to secure the compliance by them" with the provisions of the Declaration; and it was further declared that whenever the Governments of the American Republics considered it necessary they would "consult together to determine upon the measures" which they might individually or collectively undertake in order to secure the observance of the Declaration. Then followed the suggestion that, if the need to do so should arise, the American Republics might patrol the waters adjacent to their coasts, acting individually or collectively as might be agreed upon, and in so far as the means and resources of each might permit.

Basis of the claim   It is to be observed in the first place that the Declaration frankly states what is intended to be a new rule of international law.[9] The assertion of an "inherent right" on the part of the American Republics to have their continental waters free from the commission of hostile acts is not to be read as suggesting that the security zone was already in force as a rule of law. The words "inherent right" are to be taken as meaning that the American Republics believed that the new rule they were announcing was inherently reasonable and should be accepted by the belligerents for that very reason. A large part of the rules of international law have had their origin in this appeal to abstract justice; they have begun as assertions of inherent right, and in the course of time, having come to be accepted by other nations, they have acquired the character of

[9] See C. G. Fenwick, "The Declaration of Panamá," *Am. Journal of Int. Law,* XXXIV (1940), 116.

binding "legal" obligations. Such indeed, in an earlier age when multilateral treaties could not conveniently be made, was the regular way in which rules of "right reason" developed into customary law. While this means that the mere announcement of a new rule does not give it the standing of the older rules of international law acknowledged as such, the conclusion must not be drawn that nothing can be done to secure its acceptance except by way of an appeal on the ground of its reasonableness. The proponents of the new rule may obviously bring such pressure as they have at their command, within the law, to secure compliance with the rule. In the case of the Declaration of Panamá there is no reference to the use of force; and there is no ground whatever for reading a threat of force between the lines of the text.

Rejecting the suggestion of force as a "measure" for securing the compliance of the belligerents with the security zone, what other measures of a nonmilitary character are available should the belligerents not be sufficiently persuaded by a desire not to antagonize the American states? The most effective measure, and the one least open to legal objections would appear to be the denial of privileges of port to the vessels of the belligerent which refuses to comply with the provisions of the Declaration. For the privilege of admission to neutral ports is not one that the belligerents can claim as of absolute right; rather it is a concession which the neutral may grant or withhold, provided only that, if discrimination be shown, it bc based not upon an arbitrary partiality for one or other of the belligerents, but upon the desire of the neutral to protect its own national interests.

Possible measures of enforcement

In considering measures to secure observance of a claim such as is here in question it may be assumed that the American states would not expect that one of the belligerents should respect the zone while the other flagrantly violated it. It would

132

be expected that if a warship of one of the belligerents were to attack a warship of the other belligerent within the security zone, the latter would defend itself. Accepting, however, the principle of self-defense there would still remain the practical problem of determining which of the two belligerents took the initiative. This would be a question of fact, not of law.

Width of the zone   With respect to the width of the security zone, which extends to an average distance of three hundred miles, it should be observed that the American states were seeking not only to prevent hostilities so close to their shores as to endanger coastal towns and local shipping, but to prevent obstructions to inter-American communications. Hence the zone was delimited to include "all the normal maritime routes of communication and trade between the countries of America." That there might be difficulty for some of the American states in patrolling so wide a zone was recognized in the Declaration itself. But the Meeting of Foreign Ministers did not consider that ability to patrol should be a controlling factor in the case of the security zone any more than it was in the case of the marginal sea, where the immunity from hostilities was unquestioned.[10]

In its essentials the issue of the security zone represents merely another aspect of the fundamental conflict between belligerent and neutral claims. If belligerents have taken advantage of the invention of new instruments and the development of more effective methods of warfare, there is every justification for neutrals on their part to seek to limit the zones of combat and if possible, as in the case of the American Republics, to bring their collective weight to secure the peace and safety of their continental waters far remote from the immedi-

[10] See, on these aspects of the security zone, P. M. Brown, "Protective Jurisdiction," *Am. Journal of Int. Law*, XXXIV (1940), 112, where references are made to opinions justifying the extension of jurisdictional control beyond the three-mile limit.

ate theater of hostilities. The highways of commerce with
Europe have been practically closed by the belligerents. The
normally legal trade of American states with European neutrals became from the start so dangerous that many neutral
ships were unwilling to take the risk of it. In the case of the
United States trade in certain areas was even prohibited to its
citizens by law, lest in the exercise of traditional neutral rights
unfortunate incidents should occur which might arouse public
sentiment. It would seem equitable, therefore, that neutrals
should be able to draw a line about their home waters and seek
at least to protect them from becoming the scene of belligerent
operations.

The test case of the security zone came with the battle between three British cruisers and the German pocket battleship
Graf Spee on December 13, 1939.[11] Ten days later the American Republics transmitted through the President of Panamá a
joint statement protesting to France, Great Britain, and Germany against the acts which, they held, affected the neutrality
of American waters and compromised the aims of continental
protection provided for by the Declaration of Panamá.[12] The
statement went on to announce that the American states would
initiate the necessary consultation in order to "strengthen the
system of protection in common through the adoption of adequate rules" among which might be to prevent belligerent vessels from obtaining supplies and repairs in American ports
when they have committed acts of war within the security
zone.

Case of the "Graf Spee"

[11] For the case of the *Graf Spee* in relation to neutral rights under traditional law, see above, p. 58.
[12] For the text of the protest, see Department of State *Bulletin*, December
23, 1939; Pan American Union, *Law and Treaties Series*, No. 13, Supp. No.
1, p. 30.

133

Great Britain was the first to reply.[13] In a statement submitted on January 14 to the American governments through the President of Panama the British Government took note of the fact that the American Republics would not attempt to "enforce observance of the zone by unilateral action." The proposal, it said, involved "the abandonment of certain legitimate belligerent rights," which required its specific assent. This assent would depend upon an assurance that the adoption of the zone "would not provide German warships and supply ships with a vast sanctuary" from which they could emerge to attack Allied shipping and to which they could return to avoid being brought to action, and in which some unneutral service might be performed by non-German ships. Further, it would be necessary to ensure that German warships would not use the zone to pass with impunity from one ocean to the other, and that German merchant ships would not take part in inter-American trade and earn foreign exchange. The note then proceeded to repudiate the application of "sanctions" or "punitive measures" which, it held, did not "spring from the accepted canons of neutral rights and obligations." The only effective method of attaining the object of the American states would be to see that the German Government would send no more warships into the zone and that the German merchant vessels in American waters "be laid up under Pan-American control" for the duration of the war.

The French reply followed on January 23.[14] It also noted the implication that the American governments had it in mind that the constitution of such a zone, "involving a renunciation by the belligerent states of the exercise, over wide areas, of rights well established by international law," could result only from

[13] For the text, see Department of State *Bulletin,* February 24, 1940, p. 199.

[14] For the text, see *ibid.*

an agreement of all the states interested. For the rest the note repeated most of the arguments of the British note, emphasizing particularly the right of "counter attack" in view of the fact that the battle began with the attempt of the *Graf Spee* to sink the French merchant vessel *Formose* within the security zone.

The German Government had the advantage of formulating its reply in the light of the British and French replies.[15] While it noted that the proposals of the Declaration "would mean a change in existing international law," it did not "take the stand that the hitherto recognized rules of international law were bound to be regarded as a rigid and forever immutable system." Rather, these rules required adaptations to new conditions. But for the German naval vessels which had thus far been in the zone only the existing rules were applicable. The protest of December 23 was therefore not well grounded, since the zone could not be in force until accepted.

The German reply

An extraordinary argument then followed. It was said that the situation of Germany and the other belligerent powers appeared to be "disparate" in that Great Britain and France had established "possessions and bases" on the American continent and on islands offshore, and that "by these exceptions to the Monroe Doctrine in favor of Great Britain and France the effect of the security zone desired by the neutral American Governments is fundamentally and decisively impaired to start with." This "inequality" might be eliminated to a certain extent if Great Britain and France would pledge themselves not to make their possessions "starting points or bases for military operations"; but even then there would still remain the fact that Canada, a belligerent state, not only adjoined the

[15] For the text, see *ibid*. It should be noted that the translation released by the State Department differs verbally from that appearing in *The New York Times* of February 15, 1940, p. 3.

zone on the east and the west but that portions of Canada were actually surrounded by the zone. Nevertheless, it was said, a further exchange of ideas would still be in order, but for the fact that the British and French Governments had indicated that they were not willing "to take up seriously" the idea of the security zone.

Appraisal of the arguments Putting the three replies together it would seem that the insistence of the belligerents that the existing rules of international law must be regarded as in force until changed with their consent simply begs the question. The fact that the neutral American states announced it as their purpose to endeavor by joint representation to the belligerents to secure compliance by them with the Declaration is interpreted as a confession on their part that the security zone had no legal basis; whereas the correct interpretation should have been that the American states simply preferred to begin with friendly negotiation rather than with threats of economic pressure. If no change in the rules of neutrality could be made until belligerents, with their conflicting interests and with their close concentration upon immediate national purposes, gave their consent, neutrals would have no recourse but to bear with their lot, while the belligerents on their part make every change of circumstances an occasion for restricting further the rights of neutrals. What belligerent ever consulted a neutral when it extended the law of war to meet new conditions?

All three belligerents put their strongest argument upon the necessity of self-defense, that no one of them could be expected to observe the security zone while the enemy was freely violating it. The simplest answer to that would seem to be that if Great Britain and France had made their acceptance of the zone contingent upon acceptance by Germany, and vice versa, their arguments on that score would have canceled out. The British argument refers at one point to the danger lest the

zone be made a "vast sanctuary" within which German warships could hide and from which they could emerge at will to
attack British shipping. This presents a problem of neutral
duty as well as of neutral right. For it is clear that if belligerents are to renounce hostile operations within the security
zone the American Republics on their part must see to it that
the zone must not be allowed to become a base of naval operations for one belligerent against the other. This may call for a
revision of their neutrality legislation so as absolutely to ensure that no contacts be made between merchant vessels in
their ports and warships on the high seas at whatever distance
from port.[16] Without such contacts German warships would
find the zone of no value as a haven of refuge, particularly if
the doctrine of "hot pursuit" were to be accepted by the American states, permitting continuance of a battle within the zone
when begun without it.

The novel proposition of the German Government that the
American states should undertake to offset the advantage to
Great Britain and to France of their colonial possessions on
the American continent introduces a conception of neutral obligation which would call upon the neutral to readjust its entire relations with the belligerents. Neutral "impartiality" has
never been understood in that sense.[17] Neutrals have never
been required to take account of the geographical situation of
the belligerents or of the advantages which one or the other

[16] The adoption by the governments of the American Republics of the
measures recommended by the Inter-American Neutrality Committee in its
Resolution on Vessels Used as Auxiliary Transports of Warships, adopted on
February 2, 1940, would probably be adequate to secure this result. See
above, p. 128.

[17] See, on this point and on the general obligation of "impartiality," Clyde
Eagleton, "Duty of Impartiality on the Part of a Neutral," *Am. Journal of
Int. Law*, XXXIV (1940), 99.

may have from superiority of naval armaments and resulting control of the seas. The further suggestion of the German Government that the British and French possessions on the American continent constitute "exceptions to the Monroe Doctrine" is not only beside the question but historically inaccurate to the point of bewilderment.[18] But even if the American states were prepared to guarantee that the British and French Governments would not use their possessions as bases of military operations, there would still remain the hard fact, recognized in the German note, that Canada adjoins the security zone. How the American states can eject Canada from their hemisphere is more than a problem of neutrality!

One minor point in the British note deserves comment, the demand that the American states must see to it that the German merchant ships be kept from taking part in inter-American trade by which they might earn foreign exchange which might be put by the German Government to the uses of war. Here, as in the case of the German argument on colonial possessions, the neutral American states are being asked to assume obligations beyond any duty under existing law. There is no logical ground for calling upon the American states to prevent within the security zone acts of belligerent nationals which they are under no obligation to prevent being done within territorial waters. Nor has international law ever demanded of the neutral state that it prevent belligerent nationals who happen to be temporarily within its jurisdiction from earning funds that might be sent to their home country. The proposal bears all the earmarks of an effort to bargain in a case where

[18] The British, French, and Dutch possessions on and adjacent to the American continent not only antedate the proclamation of the Monroe Doctrine, but they have never been brought into question by the United States in relation to the Doctrine.

the American states owe nothing in exchange for what they
are asking.[19]

Apart from the attempt of the neutral American states to
bring their collective weight to bear in favor of the protection
of their continental waters from belligerents' operation, the
progress of the war thus far has been a record of steady encroachments by the belligerents upon the rights of neutrals.
No neutrals in the present war have been powerful enough to
threaten to strike back except only the United States which,
for reasons of its own, has chosen to abandon rights which
might involve it in controversies.[20] This inability of the neutrals to resist has had the paradoxical effect of leading to their
further punishment by one belligerent for their failure to assert effectively their rights against the other. In previous wars
the provocation would probably have been sufficient to lead
the neutral to pick the worse offender of the two and enter the
war. But the destructive potentialities of the airfleet of a
powerful belligerent have been able to intimidate most of the
neutrals, and it has been found wiser to suffer wrongs than to
fight to redress them.[21]

When the United States decided to surrender the "freedom

[19] On March 4, 1940, in response to an inquiry from the Inter-American
Neutrality Committee, the Director of the Pan American Union informed
the Committee that it was the desire of the twenty-one governments of the
American Republics that the Committee should consider the problems presented by the Declaration of Panamá and formulate recommendations both
with respect to the conditions giving rise to difficulties in the observance of
the security zone and with respect to possible methods of securing its observance on the part of the belligerents. On April 27, 1940, the Committee submitted the recommendation requested.

[20] See above, pp. 34 ff.

[21] Doubtless it would oftener be thought wiser to suffer wrongs rather
than fight to redress them, if men did not believe that acquiescence in lawlessness would sooner or later bring about conditions that would be worse
than war.

140   of the seas" rather than risk the renewal of the conditions
which had led to its entrance into the World War, there was
little hope for the small neutrals. Belligerents might well infer
that they had now a carte blanche to push to the extreme their
efforts to starve into submission an enemy they could not meet
on the field of battle.[22] Germany, as we have seen, strewed
mines in the channels of neutral commerce, until the daily
toll of neutral shipping frequently exceeded that of enemy
losses.[23] Great Britain extended its blockade of Germany so
as to include exports as well as imports; [24] and neutral protests were heeded only in so far as it seemed expedient to
Great Britain not to antagonize too far countries upon whose
good will it depended. Even Italy found it necessary to yield
to curtailment of its supplies of coal coming from Germany
by way of the sea.[25]

Retaliation   A striking instance of the retaliation by a belligerent upon
against   the smaller neutrals for the failure to assert their neutral
neutrals   rights or for yielding unduly to the demands of Great Britain
is to be seen in the threats made by Germany against neutral
vessels submitting to search in British contraband control
ports. In view of the difficulties attending the belligerent right
of visit and search at sea, neutrals had no choice but to permit themselves to be searched in the designated ports.[26] Germany gave notice to the neutrals that acquiescence on their
part would, in consequence of the opportunity afforded to Great
Britain to purchase their cargoes, be regarded as if the vessel
were bound for the British port. In the case of the Dutch vessel *Burgendijk,* which was torpedoed off the Scilly Islands by

[22] As of the date of March 25, 1940.
[23] See above, p. 74.
[24] See above, p. 86.
[25] See above, p. 87, n. 16.
[26] See above, p. 95.

a German submarine in February 14, 1940, it was reported from Berlin, some days later,[27] that an official German statement took the position that the ship's papers, even though showing neutral destination, were not decisive. For the cargo might "lose its neutral character by being made available to the enemy through entrance into an enemy port under the pretense of a prize search"; and it was unimportant for the decision of the submarine captain "whether the ship enters an enemy port of its own free will or if it is forced to enter by the enemy." It was then suggested that neutrals might "draw a lesson" whether to run into British harbors for search or not. The neutral was thus caught between Scylla and Charybdis.[28] In the case of American vessels, prohibited by national legislation from entering the designated combat zones,[29] it is interesting to imagine the legal complication which would arise if, while being conducted by a British patrol boat against its will into a control port, one of them should be torpedoed by a German submarine for yielding to duress.[30]

It would hardly be expected that the development of totalitarian governments since the World War should not have the effect of changing the application of the rules of neutrality in many important respects, in line with the changes introduced into other branches of international law. The practical identification under such governments of the individual with the

TOTALITARIAN GOVERNMENTS AND NEUTRAL RIGHTS AND DUTIES

[27] *The New York Times,* February 17, 1940, p. 3.

[28] It is difficult to credit the reports in the press of March 1, 1940, that a warning to neutrals was sent out by the German Legation at The Hague not to accept British navicerts, on the ground that although by this system neutral vessels could keep out of the danger zones they would, in accepting the navicerts, be submitting to the enemy's blockade regulations and giving the enemy opportunity to gain knowledge of business secrets.

[29] See above, p. 40.

[30] For the protest of the Department of State on this point, see Department of State *Bulletin,* January 27, 1940, p. 93.

141

142   state, the partial merging of the legal personality of the citizen with his government necessarily has made it difficult to apply as before certain rules of the law of neutrality which depended upon a distinction between what was forbidden to the government and permitted to the citizen. Already during the World War, as we have seen, the distinction between absolute and conditional contraband broke down not merely because of the development of modern systems of transportation but because of the fact that governments had now come to take over and organize the entire economic life of their peoples, so that there was no practical distinction between goods destined to the armed forces of the enemy and goods destined to the civilian population.[31] Totalitarian theories of government were not yet in effect; but, for the immediate purpose of the war, governments had even then coordinated their entire economic resources so as to bring the full power of the state to secure the most effective prosecution of the war.[32]

Effect upon distinction between the state and its citizens   Perhaps it is in respect to neutral duties that the inconsistencies between the traditional law and the new conditions resulting from the establishment of totalitarian governments may best be observed. The neutral government must be impartial, said the old law, it must maintain an equal balance in its official relations with the belligerents; it must refrain absolutely from any participation in the war, giving no help to either side; it may not even express an opinion unfriendly to one or other of the belligerents.[33] But it is not obliged to prevent its individual citizens from expressing their opinions freely; it need not prevent them from making loans, or selling arms, or in other ways contributing to the forces of one bellig-

---

[31] See above, p. 92.

[32] See on this general subject, C. G. Fenwick, *International Law* (1934), pp. 450-452.

[33] See above, p. 106.

erent as against the other.[34] The original ground for this distinction was the fact that governments simply were not able to exercise such an effective control over their citizens as to make it reasonable to call upon them to carry the neutrality of the state that far. But today a number of totalitarian governments are exercising an effective control over their citizens which would have been beyond the imagination of Frederick the Great or of Napoleon. New instruments of communication, brought under the control of the state, have not only enabled governments to exercise a vigilance hitherto unknown, but have made it possible for them to accompany the suppression of freedom of speech with positive propaganda which has tended to direct the entire thought of nations into the channels desired by the government. Under such circumstances it seems meaningless to continue to speak as if Italy, for example, could not be held responsible for statements in the public press or could not be expected to restrain its citizens from making loans or shipping arms to one or other of the belligerents.

More important than the inconsistencies in the application of the rules of neutrality resulting from the existence of totalitarian governments have been the subtle changes in the underlying principle of neutrality brought about by the formal continuance after the outbreak of hostilities of military alliances between neutrals and belligerents. The military alliance between Italy and Germany, the Rome-Berlin "axis," is still in force, whatever its terms, in spite of Italy's technical position as a neutral.[35] It is apparent that close cooperation in nonmilitary affairs is going on between the two countries, so close that if Great Britain found it expedient to do so it might well chal-

CHANGES
IN THE
THEORY OF
NEUTRALITY

[34] See above, pp. 120 ff.

[35] Mussolini is reported to have described the position of Italy as "not neutral, but merely non-belligerent." If the statement be true, we have now a new category half way between belligerents and neutrals.

lenge the neutrality of Italy according to the traditional standards. In like manner the close military cooperation between Germany and Russia in the invasion and partition of Poland, though technically short of a military alliance,[36] was clearly inconsistent with the position of technical neutrality which Russia continued to hold; and it would doubtless have been challenged by Great Britain and France if they had not desired to avoid an open break with Russia. Again on October 19, 1939, a fifteen-year "mutual assistance" pact was signed at Ankara between Great Britain, France, and Turkey, ratifications being exchanged on November 16.[37] While the pact does not contemplate military assistance except in the event of the contingencies set forth in the pact, it is difficult to reconcile its signature, while Great Britain and France were belligerents, with the standards of neutral conduct contemplated in the Hague Conventions of 1907.

NEUTRALITY NOT EVOKED BY HOSTILITIES SHORT OF "WAR"

It is a novelty of the post-World War years that certain nations should have found it desirable to resort to prolonged hostilities without recognizing themselves as formally "at war" and without claiming from third states the rights of belligerents in respect to neutral trade with the enemy or, in turn, demanding of third states the observance of neutral duties.[38]

The practice is doubtless due to the desire of the states in question, both strong powers, to avoid antagonizing more than

[36] On August 21, 1939, it was reported that Germany and Russia had signed a seven-year trade and credit agreement. This was followed on August 23 by the signing of a "non-aggression pact," ratifications (whatever they may mean) being exchanged on October 24.

[37] For the text of the pact, see *The New York Times*, October 20, 1939, p. 5.

[38] The resort to "forcible measures short of war" is of course an old practice. See C. G. Fenwick, *International Law*, Chapter XXIII. It is the scope and prolongation of the hostilities "short of war" which constitutes the legal novelty of recent years.

is necessary third states with which they have entered into obligations not to have recourse to "war," or which might resent
the restrictions put upon their trade with the weaker states
against which the hostilities are being prosecuted. In September, 1931, Japan, a signatory of the Kellogg Pact and at that
time a member of the League of Nations, invaded Manchuria;
but war was not declared against China and the normal belligerent rights in relation to blockade and contraband were not
enforced against third powers.[39] Again in July, 1937, Japan
entered upon hostilities against China without resorting to
formal war. In doing so Japan clearly violated both the Nine
Power Treaty and the Kellogg Pact.[40] But the United States
chose to overlook those aspects of the situation and to concen-
trate upon the protection of the more immediate American interests in China, in so far as they could be protected under the
circumstances. At the same time the President took advantage
of the failure of Japan to resort to formal war and did not find
that a "state of war" existed such as, if proclaimed, would
call into effect the provisions of the Neutrality Act of 1937.[41]
Doubtless it was within the power of the President to declare
that Japan's hostilities constituted a "state of war" had he desired to do so.[42] His unwillingness was apparently due to the
fact that he realized that the act would operate unequally as between China and Japan, and he did not desire to give Japan

[39] The relations of Japan's hostilities to the obligations of the Kellogg
Pact, and the doctrine on "nonrecognition" put forth by Secretary Stimson
are discussed above, p. 27.

[40] See on this point, C. G. Fenwick, "The Nine Power Treaty and the
Present Crisis in China," *Am. Journal of Int. Law*, XXXI (1937), 671.

[41] See above, p. 35.

[42] It was doubtless with this case in mind that the provision was inserted
in the law of 1939 that Congress itself might, by concurrent resolution, find
that a "state of war" existed, if the President failed to do so when Congress
thought the situation called for such action.

The case of
Finland

the advantages of it. The failure of Congress to press the matter suggested that it shared his opinion.

In December, 1939, when Russia began hostilities against Finland, the same technique of not regarding its hostilities as "war" was employed. A small number of Finns was encouraged by Russia to set up a Finnish Soviet government, which was promptly recognized by Russia as the legitimate government. The hostilities carried on by Russia against the regularly established government were, therefore, technically not "war" against Finland but merely intervention on behalf of the government which Russia had chosen to recognize as the legitimate government.

Accepting Russia's interpretation of its hostilities against Finland, the United States undertook to give direct aid to the Finns by means of a loan from the government-controlled Export-Import Bank. This would clearly have been illegal under the traditional rules of neutrality.[43] At the same time individual citizens of the United States, acting in their private capacity, made contributions and raised funds for the purchase of war material which could not be bought with the money appropriated by the Government. All these acts of individuals would, under the provisions of the Neutrality Act of 1939, immediately have become illegal if Russia had declared formal war against Finland.

[43] The fact that the loan was made by the Export-Import Bank would not of course have excused the loan had Russia chosen to declare war to hold the United States to the duties of a neutral. Under the circumstances the loan might doubtless just as well have been made by the Government itself as by its agent, the Export-Import Bank. Being made by the Bank, however, the loan had to be spent for the purchase of "surplus commodities" which it was hoped the Finns would need and which they themselves no doubt realized they could trade with other countries for war materials. The American public, it seems, dislikes at times to face realities.

VIII. CONCLUSION

The story of the struggle of the United States to maintain its rights as a neutral and to fulfill its obligations is the recital of a series of logical inconsistencies and legal contradictions. That is not due to any special failure on the part of the American Government at different periods of its history to interpret correctly the rules of international law or to abide by them honestly. Rather it is due to fundamental defects in the law of neutrality itself. It is due to the difficulty of remaining politically aloof from a conflict while at the same time being economically involved in it and emotionally affected by it. It is due to the fact that rules developed under one set of conditions have continued technically in force under wholly new conditions that sometimes have made the old rule meaningless. It is due, in consequence of these changed conditions, to the artificial distinctions that have to be put forward to justify abiding by or departing from the old rule, and to the criticism that one belligerent or the other is sure to make of the decision taken. For of this at least can the neutral be assured, that whatever stand it takes in the matter of adjusting old customs to new conditions the belligerent that is adversely affected will be prompt to put forward an accusation of failure by the neutral in its international duty.

Perhaps it might be possible to solve the logical inconsistencies in the law of neutrality if the neutral state really wanted to be neutral. But neutrality has always been in the past a

Neutrality inherently illogical

Neutral, but not too neutral

147

strain upon national emotions, and it is certainly a strain upon them at this very time. The American public clearly wants to stay out of war; it wants to be "neutral" as that policy is conceived. But the American public does not want to be *too* neutral; it does not want to be any more impartial than the law requires it to be, with a liberal interpretation of the law at that. Hence on certain minor points the American public is not only content to have its Government assert its neutral rights in principle without pressing too far in the matter of their enforcement, but would be disturbed at any other policy. Government in a democracy, for all its efforts at leadership and guidance, follows public opinion pretty closely; and public opinion, although it may unfortunately often be wrong on the facts, has an uncanny instinct for interpreting how its interests lie in the facts that are before it.

Protection of neutral rights dependent upon power to protect them

No clearer lesson is to be drawn from the history of American neutrality than that the protection of neutral rights depends upon the armed strength of the nation. When Great Powers are lined up against one another, as during the World War and in this war, weak neutrals are in a precarious position. The vicious doctrine openly proclaimed in certain quarters, that military ends justify the most ruthless means to attain those ends, makes the "law" a weak reed to lean upon. But even the strong neutral, while it may be able to ward off attacks upon its territory, may find that if it is to avoid being drawn into the war it will be called upon to sacrifice rights only less important to it than the integrity of its neutral territory. If the purpose of neutrality is to protect the position of the state which wishes to keep out of the war, then it would be a paradox indeed, as has been observed before, that the neutral state should find itself obliged to go to war to maintain its right not to go to war. Hence the neutral may find, as the United States has found, that it is wiser to abandon certain neutral rights, no matter how well established they may be, than to risk the possibility of incidents arising that might inflame public opinion and lead it, in a moment of national excitement, to use force to protect its violated rights. Just where the line is to be drawn, between rights that the strong neutral will defend at the risk of war and rights that are not worth fighting for in a world in which there are so many better causes to fight for, is a problem of statesmanship which no hard and fast rules of neutrality can solve.

But if the integrity of neutral rights depends upon the military power of the neutral state and not upon the law-abiding attitude of the belligerents, it is to be hoped that American public opinion will in time come to see that it would be the part of prudence to use that same power of the United States to prevent war rather than to be indifferent to the conditions leading to war, and then, when it has come, try to maintain a policy of neutrality towards it. The most rigorously neutral policy that could be maintained will not prevent the United States from feeling the effects of the moral and economic ruin that is certain to come in the wake of war. Nations that have exhausted themselves in a life and death struggle cannot easily return to the processes of orderly constitutional government, or maintain democratic ideals of freedom, or uphold the conceptions of law and justice based upon the triumph of reason over force. Violence has an unhappy way of begetting violence, and the morality of Christendom will inevitably suffer for a time from the shock. Nor can there be much promise of friendly and mutually beneficial commercial relations between countries whose domestic economies have been thrown out of gear by war and whose immediate national interest at the close of this war will almost inevitably seem to them to lie in policies of economic nationalism, under which free enterprise will have small chance of revival.

Use of power
to prevent
war

True criticism of neutrality

Fundamentally the problem of neutrality is the result of an unorganized community of nations. The true criticism of it is not that it may not be the best policy to pursue when war has actually broken out and it is too late to restore order without increasing the spread of the conflagration. Rather the criticism of it must be directed against the pre-war policies of the nation which, seeing an impending catastrophe, found no way to avert it while there was yet time. It is the unwillingness to cooperate in the development of legal standards by which the conduct of nations may be judged, and the refusal to issue a warning in advance that the outlaw who flaunts these standards and attacks his neighbor will not be treated on a par with his victim, it is this "neutrality" in time of peace that is to be condemned. Obviously a weak state is not in a position to take such a stand without the support of the other members of the community; for it cannot be expected to risk its national existence in an effort to uphold the principle of law and order. Only the strongest of the powers can take such action individually; and it is clear that if such a power could act in cooperation with other law-abiding powers their combined efforts might constitute such predominant power that the potential outlaw could be restrained without recourse to actual force.

Whether, in the world which will follow the present war, even the fullest cooperation on the part of the United States with other law-abiding nations will succeed in creating a stable community of nations and in developing rules of law that can be enforced by the collective will of the community cannot be affirmed with absolute certainty. For the effectiveness of such cooperation will depend in large part upon the state of public morality when that time comes. If the international law of the future is to be conceived in terms of suppressing violence without reference to the conditions that make for violence, if international order is to consist merely in the maintenance of the *status quo* for those that are favored by it, if no provision is to be made for "peaceful change" as the alternative to recourse to methods of force, if "justice" is to be conceived of in terms of duty to the citizens of one's own country without reference to the needs of the people of other countries—then, indeed, all efforts at international cooperation must inevitably fail for want of any fundamental common purpose on the part of the nations pretending to cooperate.

The outlook for a stable international order is, therefore, bright or dark, as we would have it. Cooperation is doomed to failure if it limits its objectives and does not undertake the most rigorous examination of the causes of war. But it offers good prospect of success if undertaken in a more generous spirit. A moral basis for international unity must be found; law and justice must be made international as well as national conceptions; and the welfare of the whole community of nations must be conceived of as an objective of national policies. The task may well be a more difficult one than it would have been in 1920. But the greater difficulty of the task only constitutes a challenge to those who realize how urgent is the need of undertaking it.

The United States has a vital national interest in the maintenance of international law and order. That interest is not incidental to any lesser interest; it is a primary interest in itself. It is not a transitory or occasional interest, to be considered when an emergency arises and then abandoned in times of comparative calm. It is a fundamental interest which of necessity results from the fact that we are living in a world with other nations and cannot cut ourselves off from social and economic relations with them, no matter what degree of formal political detachment we may endeavor to maintain. We have a right to protect that interest against lawbreakers; and we have a duty to protect it. For there can be no more than an

Interest of the United States in international law and order

152   armed peace ahead of us for many years to come unless we are willing to undertake with other nations the formulation of just rules of law and also willing, when they have been formulated, to cooperate in maintaining them.

APPENDIX A

PROCLAMATION OF NEUTRALITY OF THE UNITED STATES,
SEPTEMBER 5, 1939 [1]

BY THE PRESIDENT OF THE UNITED STATES
OF AMERICA

A PROCLAMATION [No. 2348]

Whereas a state of war unhappily exists between Germany and France; Poland; and the United Kingdom, India, Australia and New Zealand; [2]

And whereas the United States is on terms of friendship and amity with the contending powers, and with the persons inhabiting their several dominions;

And whereas there are nationals of the United States residing within the territories or dominions of each of the said belligerents, and carrying on commerce, trade, or other business or pursuits therein;

[1] A note prefixed by the State Department calls attention to the confusion caused by the two separate proclamations issued on the same day, this first proclamation having to do with the activities of the United States as a neutral "under the rules and procedure of international law, and those of our domestic statutes in harmony therewith." The second proclamation brought into effect the provisions of the Joint Resolution of May 1, 1937. This proclamation was revoked by the proclamation (No. 2374) bringing into effect the Joint Resolution of November 4, 1939. See below, p. 164.

[2] By proclamation of September 8 and 10, 1939, the Union of South Africa and Canada were added to the list.

And whereas there are nationals of each of the said belligerents residing within the territory or jurisdiction of the United States, and carrying on commerce, trade, or other business or pursuits therein;

And whereas the laws and treaties of the United States, without interfering with the free expression of opinion and sympathy, nevertheless impose upon all persons who may be within their territory and jurisdiction the duty of an impartial neutrality during the existence of the contest;

And whereas it is the duty of a neutral government not to permit or suffer the making of its territory or territorial waters subservient to the purposes of war;

Now, therefore, I, Franklin D. Roosevelt, President of the United States of America, in order to preserve the neutrality of the United States and of its citizens and of persons within its territory and jurisdiction, and to enforce its laws and treaties, and in order that all persons, being warned of the general tenor of the laws and treaties of the United States in this behalf, and of the law of nations, may thus be prevented from any violation of the same, do hereby declare and proclaim that by certain provisions of the act approved on the 4th day of March, A. D. 1909, commonly known as the "Penal Code of the United States" and of the act approved on the 15th day of June, A. D. 1917, the following acts are forbidden to be done, under severe penalties, within the territory and jurisdiction of the United States, to wit:

1. Accepting and exercising a commission to serve one of the said belligerents by land or by sea against an opposing belligerent.

2. Enlisting or entering into the service of a belligerent as a soldier, or as a marine, or seaman on board of any ship of war, letter of marque, or privateer.

3. Hiring or retaining another person to enlist or enter himself in the service of a belligerent as a soldier, or as a marine, or seaman on board of any ship of war, letter of marque, or privateer.

4. Hiring another person to go beyond the limits or jurisdiction of the United States with intent to be enlisted as aforesaid.

5. Hiring another person to go beyond the limits or jurisdiction of the United States with intent to be entered into service as aforesaid.

6. Retaining another person to go beyond the limits or jurisdiction of the United States to be enlisted as aforesaid.

7. Retaining another person to go beyond the limits or jurisdiction of the United States with intent to be entered into service as aforesaid. (But the said act of the 4th day of March, A. D. 1909, as amended by the act of the 15th day of June, A. D. 1917, is not to be construed to extend to a citizen or subject of a belligerent who, being transiently within the jurisdiction of the United States, shall, on board of any ship of war, which, at the time of its arrival within the jurisdiction of the United States, was fitted and equipped as such ship of war, enlist or enter himself or hire or retain another subject or citizen of the same belligerent, who is transiently within the jurisdiction of the United States, to enlist or enter himself to serve such belligerent on board such ship of war, if the United States shall then be at peace with such belligerent.)

8. Fitting out and arming, or attempting to fit out and arm, or procuring to be fitted out and armed, or knowingly being concerned in the furnishing, fitting out, or arming of any ship or vessel with intent that such ship or vessel shall be employed in the service of one of the said belligerents to cruise, or commit hostilities against the subjects, citizens, or property of an opposing belligerent.

9. Issuing or delivering a commission within the territory or jurisdiction of the United States for any ship or vessel to the intent that she may be employed as aforesaid.

10. Increasing or augmenting, or procuring to be increased or augmented, or knowingly being concerned in increasing or augmenting, the force of any ship of war, cruiser, or other armed vessel, which at the time of her arrival within the jurisdiction of

the United States was a ship of war, cruiser, or armed vessel in the service of a belligerent, or belonging to a national thereof, by adding to the number of guns of such vessel, or by changing those on board of her for guns of a larger caliber, or by the addition thereto of any equipment solely applicable to war.

11. Knowingly beginning or setting on foot or providing or preparing a means for or furnishing the money for, or taking part in, any military or naval expedition or enterprise to be carried on from the territory or jurisdiction of the United States against the territory or dominion of a belligerent.

12. Despatching from the United States, or any place subject to the jurisdiction thereof, any vessel, domestic or foreign, which is about to carry to a warship, tender, or supply ship of a belligerent any fuel, arms, ammunition, men, supplies, despatches, or information shipped or received on board within the jurisdiction of the United States.

13. Despatching from the United States, or any place subject to the jurisdiction thereof, any armed vessel owned wholly or in part by American citizens, or any vessel, domestic or foreign (other than one which has entered the jurisdiction of the United States as a public vessel), which is manifestly built for warlike purposes or has been converted or adapted from a private vessel to one suitable for warlike use, and which is to be employed to cruise against or commit or attempt to commit hostilities upon the subjects, citizens, or property of a belligerent nation, or which will be sold or delivered to a belligerent nation, or to an agent, officer, or citizen thereof, within the jurisdiction of the United States, or, having left that jurisdiction, upon the high seas.

14. Despatching from the United States, or any place subject to the jurisdiction thereof, any vessel built, armed, or equipped as a ship of war, or converted from a private vessel into a ship of war (other than one which has entered the jurisdiction of the United States as a public vessel), with any intent or under any agreement or contract, written or oral, that such vessel shall be delivered to

a belligerent nation, or to any agent, officer, or citizen of such nation, or where there is reasonable cause to believe that the said vessel shall or will be employed in the service of such belligerent nation after its departure from the jurisdiction of the United States.

15. Taking, or attempting or conspiring to take, or authorizing the taking of any vessel out of port or from the jurisdiction of the United States in violation of the said act of the 15th day of June, A. D. 1917, as set forth in the preceding paragraphs numbered 11 to 14 inclusive.

16. Leaving or attempting to leave the jurisdiction of the United States by a person belonging to the armed land or naval forces of a belligerent who shall have been interned within the jurisdiction of the United States in accordance with the law of nations, or leaving or attempting to leave the limits of internment in which freedom of movement has been allowed, without permission from the proper official of the United States in charge, or wilfully overstaying a leave of absence granted by such official.

17. Aiding or enticing any interned person to escape or attempt to escape from the jurisdiction of the United States, or from the limits of internment prescribed.

And I do hereby further declare and proclaim that any frequenting and use of the waters within the territorial jurisdiction of the United States by the vessels of a belligerent, whether public ships or privateers for the purpose of preparing for hostile operations, or as posts of observation upon the ships of war or privateers or merchant vessels of an opposing belligerent must be regarded as unfriendly and offensive, and in violation of that neutrality which it is the determination of this government to observe; and to the end that the hazard and inconvenience of such apprehended practices may be avoided, I further proclaim and declare that from and after the fifth day of September instant, and so long as this proclamation shall be in effect, no ship of war or privateer of any belligerent shall be permitted to make use of any port, harbor, roadstead, or waters subject to the jurisdiction of the United States as a station or place of resort for any warlike purpose or for the purpose of obtaining warlike equipment; no privateer of a belligerent shall be permitted to depart from any port, harbor, roadstead, or waters subject to the jurisdiction of the United States; and no ship of war of a belligerent shall be permitted to sail out of or leave any port, harbor, roadstead, or waters subject to the jurisdiction of the United States from which a vessel of an opposing belligerent (whether the same shall be a ship of war or a merchant ship) shall have previously departed, until after the expiration of at least twenty-four hours from the departure of such last mentioned vessel beyond the jurisdiction of the United States.

If any ship of war of a belligerent shall, after the time this notification takes effect, be found in, or shall enter any port, harbor, roadstead, or waters subject to the jurisdiction of the United States, such vessel shall not be permitted to remain in such port, harbor, roadstead, or waters more than twenty-four hours, except in case of stress of weather, or for delay in receiving supplies or repairs, or when detained by the United States; in any of which cases the authorities of the port, or of the nearest port (as the case may be), shall require her to put to sea as soon as the cause of the delay is at an end, unless within the preceding twenty-four hours a vessel, whether ship of war or merchant ship of an opposing belligerent, shall have departed therefrom in which case the time limited for the departure of such ship of war shall be extended so far as may be necessary to secure an interval of not less than twenty-four hours between such departure and that of any ship of war or merchant ship of an opposing belligerent which may have previously quit the same port, harbor, roadstead, or waters.

Vessels used exclusively for scientific, religious, or philanthropic purposes are exempted from the foregoing provisions as to the length of time ships of war may remain in the ports, harbors, roadsteads, or waters subject to the jurisdiction of the United States.

The maximum number of ships of war belonging to a belligerent and its allies which may be in one of the ports, harbors, or roadsteads subject to the jurisdiction of the United States simultaneously shall be three.

When ships of war of opposing belligerents are present simultaneously in the same port, harbor, roadstead, or waters, subject to the jurisdiction of the United States, the one entering first shall depart first, unless she is in such condition as to warrant extending her stay. In any case the ship which arrived later has the right to notify the other through the competent local authority that within twenty-four hours she will leave such port, harbor, roadstead, or waters, the one first entering, however, having the right to depart within that time. If the one first entering leaves, the notifying ship must observe the prescribed interval of twenty-four hours. If a delay beyond twenty-four hours from the time of arrival is granted, the termination of the cause of delay will be considered the time of arrival in deciding the right of priority in departing.

Vessels of a belligerent shall not be permitted to depart successively from any port, harbor, roadstead, or waters subject to the jurisdiction of the United States at such intervals as will delay the departure of a ship of war of an opposing belligerent from such ports, harbors, roadsteads, or waters for more than twenty-four hours beyond her desired time of sailing. If, however, the departure of several ships of war and merchant ships of opposing belligerents from the same port, harbor, roadstead, or waters is involved, the order of their departure therefrom shall be so arranged as to afford the opportunity of leaving alternately to the vessels of the opposing belligerents, and to cause the least detention consistent with the objects of this proclamation.

All belligerent vessels shall refrain from use of their radio and signal apparatus while in the harbors, ports, roadsteads, or waters subject to the jurisdiction of the United States, except for calls of distress and communications connected with safe navigation or arrangements for the arrival of the vessel within, or departure from, such harbors, ports, roadsteads, or waters, or passage through such waters; provided that such communications will not be of direct material aid to the belligerent in the conduct of military operations against an opposing belligerent. The radio of belligerent merchant vessels may be sealed by the authorities of the United States, and such seals shall not be broken within the jurisdiction of the United States except by proper authority of the United States.

No ship of war of a belligerent shall be permitted, while in any port, harbor, roadstead, or waters subject to the jurisdiction of the United States, to take in any supplies except provisions and such other things as may be requisite for the subsistence of her crew in amounts necessary to bring such supplies to her peace standard, and except such fuel, lubricants, and feed water only as may be sufficient, with that already on board, to carry such vessel, if without any sail power, to the nearest port of her own country; or in case a vessel is rigged to go under sail, and may also be propelled by machinery, then half the quantity of fuel, lubricants, and feed water which she would be entitled to have on board, if dependent upon propelling machinery alone, and no fuel, lubricants, or feed water shall be again supplied to any such ship of war in the same or any other port, harbor, roadstead, or waters subject to the jurisdiction of the United States until after the expiration of three months from the time when such fuel, lubricants and feed water may have been last supplied to her within waters subject to the jurisdiction of the United States. The amounts of fuel, lubricants, and feed water allowable under the above provisions shall be based on the economical speed of the vessel, plus an allowance of thirty per centum for eventualities.

No ship of war of a belligerent shall be permitted, while in any port, harbor, roadstead, or waters subject to the jurisdiction of the United States, to make repairs beyond those that are essential to render the vessel seaworthy and which in no degree constitute an

increase in her military strength. Repairs shall be made without
delay. Damages which are found to have been produced by the enemy's fire shall in no case be repaired.

No ship of war of a belligerent shall effect repairs or receive fuel, lubricants, feed water, or provisions within the jurisdiction of the United States without written authorization of the proper authorities of the United States. Before such authorization will be issued, the commander of the vessel shall furnish to such authorities a written declaration, duly signed by such commander, stating the date, port, and amounts of supplies last received in the jurisdiction of the United States, the amounts of fuel, lubricants, feed water, and provisions on board, the port to which the vessel is proceeding, the economical speed of the vessel, the rate of consumption of fuel, lubricants, and feed water at such speed, and the amount of each class of supplies desired. If repairs are desired, a similar declaration shall be furnished stating the cause of the damage and the nature of the repairs. In either case, a certificate shall be included to the effect that the desired services are in accord with the rules of the United States in that behalf.

No agency of the United States Government shall, directly or indirectly, provide supplies nor effect repairs to a belligerent ship of war.

No vessel of a belligerent shall exercise the right of search within the waters under the jurisdiction of the United States, nor shall prizes be taken by belligerent vessels within such waters. Subject to any applicable treaty provisions in force, prizes captured by belligerent vessels shall not enter any port, harbor, roadstead, or waters under the jurisdiction of the United States except in case of unseaworthiness, stress of weather, or want of fuel or provisions; when the cause has disappeared, the prize must leave immediately, and if a prize captured by a belligerent vessel enters any port, harbor, roadstead, or waters subject to the jurisdiction of the United States for any other reason than on account of unseaworthiness, stress of weather, or want of fuel or provisions, or fails to leave as soon as the circumstances which justified the entrance are at an end, the prize with its officers and crew will be released and the prize crew will be interned. A belligerent Prize Court can not be set up on territory subject to the jurisdiction of the United States or on a vessel in the ports, harbors, roadsteads, or waters subject to the jurisdiction of the United States.

The provisions of this proclamation pertaining to ships of war shall apply equally to any vessel operating under public control for hostile or military purposes.

And I do further declare and proclaim that the statutes and the treaties of the United States and the law of nations alike require that no person, within the territory and jurisdiction of the United States, shall take part, directly or indirectly, in the said war, but shall remain at peace with all of the said belligerents, and shall maintain a strict and impartial neutrality.

And I do further declare and proclaim that the provisions of this proclamation shall apply to the Canal Zone except in so far as such provisions may be specifically modified by a proclamation or proclamations issued for the Canal Zone.

And I do hereby enjoin all nationals of the United States, and all persons residing or being within the territory or jurisdiction of the United States, to observe the laws thereof, and to commit no act contrary to the provisions of the said statutes or treaties or in violation of the law of nations in that behalf.

And I do hereby give notice that all nationals of the United States and others who may claim the protection of this government, who may misconduct themselves in the premises, will do so at their peril, and that they can in no wise obtain any protection from the government of the United States against the consequences of their misconduct.

This proclamation shall continue in full force and effect unless and until modified, revoked or otherwise terminated, pursuant to law.

In witness whereof, I have hereunto set my hand and caused the 163
seal of the United States to be affixed.

Done at the city of Washington this fifth day of September in
the year of our Lord nineteen hundred and thirty-
(SEAL) nine, and of the Independence of the United States
of America the one hundred and sixty-fourth.

By the President:

FRANKLIN D. ROOSEVELT

CORDELL HULL
Secretary of State.

APPENDIX B

The Neutrality Act of 1939

(PUBLIC RESOLUTION—No. 54—SEVENTY-SIXTH CONGRESS, SECOND SESSION)

JOINT RESOLUTION: TO PRESERVE THE NEUTRALITY AND THE PEACE OF THE UNITED STATES AND TO SECURE THE SAFETY OF ITS CITIZENS AND THEIR INTERESTS, APPROVED NOVEMBER 4, 1939.

Whereas the United States, desiring to preserve its neutrality in wars between foreign states and desiring also to avoid involvement therein, voluntarily imposes upon its nationals by domestic legislation the restrictions set out in this joint resolution; and

Whereas by so doing the United States waives none of its own rights or privileges, or those of any of its nationals, under international law, and expressly reserves all the rights and privileges to which it and its nationals are entitled under the law of nations; and

Whereas the United States hereby expressly reserves the right to repeal, change or modify this joint resolution or any other domestic legislation in the interests of the peace, security or welfare of the United States and its people: Therefore be it

Resolved by the Senate and House of Representatives of the United States of America in Congress assembled,

Section 1. (a) That whenever the President, or the Congress by concurrent resolution, shall find that there exists a state of war between foreign states, and that it is necessary to promote the security or preserve the peace of the United States or to protect the lives of citizens of the United States, the President shall issue a proclamation naming the states involved; and he shall, from time to time, by proclamation, name other states as and when they may become involved in the war.

(b) Whenever the state of war which shall have caused the President to issue any proclamation under the authority of this section shall have ceased to exist with respect to any state named in such proclamation, he shall revoke such proclamation with respect to such state.

COMMERCE WITH STATES ENGAGED IN ARMED CONFLICT

Section 2. (a) Whenever the President shall have issued a proclamation under the authority of. section 1 (a) it shall thereafter be unlawful for any American vessel to carry any passengers or any articles or materials to any state named in such proclamation.

(b) Whoever shall violate any of the provisions of subsection (a) of this section or of any regulations issued thereunder shall, upon conviction thereof, be fined not more than $50,000 or imprisoned for not more than five years, or both. Should the violation be by a corporation, organization, or association, each officer or director thereof participating in the violation shall be liable to the penalty herein prescribed.

(c) Whenever the President shall have issued a proclamation under the authority of section 1 (a) it shall thereafter be unlawful to export or transport, or attempt to export or transport, or cause to be exported or transported, from the United States to any state named in such proclamation, any articles or materials (except copyrighted articles or materials) until all right, title, and interest therein shall have been transferred to some foreign government, agency, institution, association, partnership, corporation, or national. Issuance of a bill of lading under which title to the articles or materials to be exported or transported passes to a foreign purchaser unconditionally upon the delivery of such articles or materials to a carrier, shall constitute a transfer of all right, title, and interest therein within the meaning of this subsection. The shipper of such articles or materials shall be required to file with the collector of the port from or through which they are to be exported a declaration under oath that he has complied with the requirements of this subsection with respect to transfer of right, title, and interest in such articles or materials, and that he will comply with such rules and regulations as shall be promulgated from time to time. Any such declaration so filed shall be a conclusive estoppel against any claim of any citizen of the United States of right, title, or interest in such articles or materials, if such citizen had knowledge of the filing of such declaration; and the exportation or transportation of any articles or materials without filing the declaration required by this subsection shall be a conclusive estoppel against any claim of any citizen of the United States of right, title, or interest in such articles or materials, if such citizen had knowledge of such violation. No loss incurred by any such citizen (1) in connection with the sale or transfer of right, title, and interest in any such articles or materials or (2) in connection with the exportation or transportation of any such copyrighted articles or materials shall be made the basis of any claim put forward by the Government of the United States.

(d) Insurance written by underwriters on articles or materials included in shipments which are subject to restrictions under the provisions of this joint resolution, and on vessels carrying such shipments shall not be deemed an American interest therein, and no insurance policy issued on such articles or materials, or vessels,

and no loss incurred thereunder or by the owners of such vessels,
shall be made the basis of any claim put forward by the Government of the United States.

(e) Whenever any proclamation issued under the authority of section 1 (a) shall have been revoked with respect to any state the provisions of this section shall thereupon cease to apply with respect to such state, except as to offenses committed prior to such revocation.

(f) The provisions of subsection (a) of this section shall not apply to transportation by American vessels on or over lakes, rivers, and inland waters bordering on the United States, or to transportation by aircraft on or over land bordering on the United States; and the provisions of subsection (c) of this section shall not apply (1) to such transportation of any articles or materials other than articles listed in a proclamation referred to in or issued under the authority of section 12 (i), or (2) to any other transportation on or over lands bordering on the United States of any articles or materials other than articles listed in a proclamation referred to in or issued under the authority of section 12 (i); and the provisions of subsections (a) and (c) of this section shall not apply to the transportation referred to in this subsection and subsections (g) and (h) of any articles or materials listed in a proclamation referred to in or issued under the authority of section 12 (i) if the articles or materials so listed are to be used exclusively by American vessels, aircraft, or other vehicles in connection with their operation and maintenance.

(g) The provisions of subsections (a) and (c) of this section shall not apply to transportation by American vessels (other than aircraft) of mail, passengers, or any articles or materials (except articles or materials listed in a proclamation referred to in or issued under the authority of section 12 (i)) (1) to any port in the Western Hemisphere south of thirty-five degrees north latitude, (2) to any port in the Western Hemisphere north of thirty-five degrees north latitude and west of sixty-six degrees west longitude,

(3) to any port on the Pacific or Indian Oceans, including the China Sea, the Tasman Sea, the Bay of Bengal, and the Arabian Sea, and any other dependent waters of either of such oceans, seas, or bays, or (4) to any port on the Atlantic Ocean or its dependent waters south of thirty degrees north latitude. The exceptions contained in this subsection shall not apply to any such port which is included within a combat area as defines in section 3 which applies to such vessels.

(h) The provisions of subsections (a) and (c) of this section shall not apply to transportation by aircraft of mail, passengers, or any articles or materials (except articles or materials listed in a proclamation referred to in or issued under the authority of Section 12 (i)) (1) to any port in the Western Hemisphere, or (2) to any port on the Pacific or Indian Oceans, including the China Sea, the Tasman Sea, the Bay of Bengal, and the Arabian Sea, and any other dependent waters of either of such oceans, seas, or bays. The exceptions contained in this subsection shall not apply to any such port which is included within a combat area as defined in section 3 which applies to such aircraft.

(i) Every American vessel to which the provisions of subsections (g) and (h) apply, and every neutral vessel to which the provisions of subsection (1) apply, shall, before departing from a port or from the jurisdiction of the United States, file with the collector of customs of the port of departure, or if there is no such collector at such port then with the nearest collector of customs, a sworn statement (1) containing a complete list of all the articles and materials carried as cargo by such vessel, and the names and addresses of the consignees of all such articles and materials, and (2) stating the ports at which such articles and materials are to be unloaded and the ports of call of such vessel. All transportation referred to in subsections (f), (g), (h), and (1) of this section shall be subject to such restrictions, rules, and regulations as the President shall prescribe; but no loss incurred in connection with any transportation excepted under the provisions of subsections (g), (h), and (1) of this section shall be made the basis of any claim put forward by the Government of the United States.

(j) Whenever all proclamations issued under the authority of section 1 (a) shall have been revoked, the provisions of subsections (f), (g), (h), (i), and (1) of this section shall expire.

(k) The provisions of this section shall not apply to the current voyage of any American vessel which has cleared for a foreign port and has departed from a port or from the jurisdiction of the United States in advance of (1) the date of enactment of this joint resolution, or (2) any proclamation issued after such date under the authority of section 1 (a) of this joint resolution; but any such vessel shall proceed at its own risk after either of such dates, and no loss incurred in connection with any such vessel or its cargo after either of such dates shall be made the basis of any claim put forward by the Government of the United States.

(1) The provisions of subsection (c) of this section shall not apply to the transportation by a neutral vessel to any port referred to in subsection (g) of this section of any articles or materials (except articles or materials listed in a proclamation referred to in or issued under the authority of section 12 (i)) so long as such port is not included within a combat area as defined in section 3 which applies to American vessels.

COMBAT AREAS

Section 3. (a) Whenever the President shall have issued a proclamation under the authority of section 1 (a), and he shall thereafter find that the protection of citizens of the United States so requires, he shall, by proclamation, define combat areas, and thereafter it shall be unlawful, except under such rules and regulations as may be prescribed, for any citizen of the United States or any American vessel to proceed into or through any such combat area. The combat areas so defined may be made to apply to surface vessels or aircraft, or both.

(b) In case of the violation of any of the provisions of this section by any American vessel, or any owner or officer thereof, such vessel, owner, or officer shall be fined not more than $50,000 or imprisoned for not more than five years, or both. Should the owner of such vessel be a corporation, organization, or association, each officer or director participating in the violation shall be liable to the penalty hereinabove prescribed. In case of the violation of this section by any citizen traveling as a passenger, such passenger may be fined not more than $10,000 or imprisoned for not more than two years, or both.

(c) The President may from time to time modify or extend any proclamation issued under the authority of this section, and when the conditions which shall have caused him to issue any such proclamation shall have ceased to exist he shall revoke such proclamation and the provisions of this section shall thereupon cease to apply, except as to offenses committed prior to such revocation.

AMERICAN RED CROSS

Section 4. The provisions of section 2 (a) shall not prohibit the transportation by vessels under charter or other direction and control of the American Red Cross, proceeding under safe conduct granted by states ·named in any proclamation issued under the authority of section 1 (a), of officers and American Red Cross personnel, medical personnel, and medical supplies, food, and clothing, for the relief of human suffering.

TRAVEL ON VESSELS OF BELLIGERENT STATES

Section 5. (a) Whenever the President shall have issued a proclamation under the authority of section 1 (a) it shall thereafter be unlawful for any citizen of the United States to travel on any vessel of any state named in such proclamation, except in accordance with such rules and regulations as may be prescribed.

(b) Whenever any proclamation issued under the authority of

section 1 (a) shall have been revoked with respect to any state the provisions of this section shall thereupon cease to apply with respect to such state, except as to offenses committed prior to such revocation.

ARMING OF AMERICAN MERCHANT VESSELS PROHIBITED

Section 6. Whenever the President shall have issued a proclamation under the authority of section 1 (a), it shall thereafter be unlawful, until such proclamation is revoked, for any American vessel, engaged in commerce with any foreign state to be armed, except with small arms and ammunition therefor, which the President may deem necessary and shall publicly designate for the preservation of discipline aboard any such vessel.

FINANCIAL TRANSACTIONS

Section 7. (a) Whenever the President shall have issued a proclamation under the authority of section 1 (a), it shall thereafter be unlawful for any person within the United States to purchase, sell, or exchange bonds, securities, or other obligations of the government of any state named in such proclamation, or of any political subdivision of any such state, or of any person acting for or on behalf of the government of any such state, or political subdivision thereof, issued after the date of such proclamation, or to make any loan or extend any credit (other than necessary credits accruing in connection with the transmission of telegraph, cable, wireless and telephone services) to any such government, political subdivision, or person. The provisions of this subsection shall also apply to the sale by any person within the United States to any person in a state named in any such proclamation of any articles or materials listed in a proclamation referred to in or issued under the authority of section 12 (i).

(b) The provisions of this section shall not apply to a renewal or adjustment of such indebtedness as may exist on the date of such proclamation.

(c) Whoever shall knowingly violate any of the provisions of this section or of any regulations issued thereunder shall, upon conviction thereof, be fined not more than $50,000 or imprisoned for not more than five years, or both. Should the violation be by a corporation, organization, or association, each officer or director thereof participating in the violation shall be liable to the penalty herein prescribed.

(d) Whenever any proclamation issued under the authority of section 1 (a) shall have been revoked with respect to any state the provisions of this section shall thereupon cease to apply with respect to such state, except as to offenses committed prior to such revocations.

SOLICITATION AND COLLECTION OF FUNDS AND CONTRIBUTIONS

Section 8. (a) Whenever the President shall have issued a proclamation under the authority of section 1 (a), it shall thereafter be unlawful for any person within the United States to solicit or receive any contribution for or on behalf of the government of any state named in such proclamation or for or on behalf of any agent or instrumentality of any such state.

(b) Nothing in this section shall be construed to prohibit the solicitation or collection of funds and contributions to be used for medical aid and assistance, or for food and clothing to relieve human suffering, when such solicitation or collection of funds and contributions is made on behalf of and for use by any person or organization which is not acting for or on behalf of any such government, but all such solicitations and collections of funds and contributions shall be in accordance with and subject to such rules and regulations as may be prescribed.

(c) Whenever any proclamation issued under the authority of section 1 (a) shall have been revoked with respect to any state the provisions of this section shall thereupon cease to apply with respect to such state, except as to offenses committed prior to such revocation.

AMERICAN REPUBLICS

Section 9. This joint resolution (except section 12) shall not apply to any American Republic engaged in war against a non-American state or states, provided the American republic is not cooperating with a non-American state or states in such war.

RESTRICTIONS ON USE OF AMERICAN PORTS

Section 10. (a) Whenever, during any war in which the United States is neutral, the President, or any person thereunto authorized by him, shall have cause to believe that any vessel, domestic or foreign, whether requiring clearance or not, is about to carry out of a port or from the jurisdiction of the United States, fuel, men, arms, ammunition, implements of war, supplies, dispatches, or information to any warship, tender, or supply ship of a state named in a proclamation issued under the authority of section 1 (a), but the evidence is not deemed sufficient to justify forbidding the departure of the vessel as provided for by section 1, title V, chapter 30, of the Act approved June 15, 1917 (40 Stat. 217. 221; U.S.C., 1934 edition, title 18, sec. 31), and if, in the President's judgment, such action will serve to maintain peace between the United States and foreign states, or to protect the commercial interests of the United States and its citizens, or to promote the security or neutrality of the United States, he shall have the power, and it shall be his duty to require the owner, master, or person in command thereof, before departing from a port or from the jurisdiction of the United States, to give a bond to the United States, with sufficient sureties, in such amount as he shall deem proper, conditioned that the vessel will not deliver the men, or any fuel, supplies, dispatches, information, or any part of the cargo, to any warship, tender, or supply ship of a state named in a proclamation issued under the authority of section 1 (a).

(b) If the President, or any person thereunto authorized by him, shall find that a vessel, domestic or foreign, in a port of the United States, has previously departed from a port or from the jurisdiction of the United States during such war and delivered men, fuel, supplies, dispatches, information, or any part of its cargo to a warship, tender, or supply ship of a state named in a proclamation issued under the authority of section 1 (a), he may prohibit the departure of such vessel during the duration of the war.

(c) Whenever the President shall have issued a proclamation under section 1 (a) he may, while such proclamation is in effect, require the owner, master, or person in command of any vessel, foreign or domestic, before departing from the United States, to give a bond to the United States, with sufficient sureties, in such amount as he shall deem proper, conditioned that no alien seaman who arrived on such vessel shall remain in the United States for a longer period than that permitted under the regulations, as amended from time to time, issued pursuant to section 33 of the Immigration Act of February 5, 1917 (U.S.C., title 8, sec. 168). Notwithstanding the provisions of said section 33, the President may issue such regulations with respect to the landing of such seamen as he deems necessary to insure their departure either on such vessel or another vessel at the expense of such owner, master, or person in command.

SUBMARINES AND ARMED MERCHANT VESSELS

Section 11. Whenever, during any war in which the United States is neutral, the President shall find that special restrictions placed on the use of the ports and territorial waters of the United States by the submarines or armed merchant vessels of a foreign state will serve to maintain peace between the United States and foreign states, or to protect the commercial interests of the United

States and its citizens, or to promote the security of the United States, and shall make proclamation thereof, it shall thereafter be unlawful for any such submarine or armed merchant vessel to enter a port or the territorial waters of the United States or to depart therefrom, except under such conditions and subject to such limitations as the President may prescribe. Whenever, in his judgment, the conditions which have caused him to issue his proclamation have ceased to exist, he shall revoke his proclamation and the provisions of this section shall thereupon cease to apply, except as to offenses committed prior to such revocation.

NATIONAL MUNITIONS CONTROL BOARD

Section 12. (a) There is hereby established a National Munitions Control Board (hereinafter referred to as the "Board"). The Board shall consist of the Secretary of State, who shall be chairman and executive officer of the Board, the Secretary of the Treasury, the Secretary of War, the Secretary of the Navy, and the Secretary of Commerce. Except as otherwise provided in this section, or by other law, the administration of this section is vested in the Secretary of State. The Secretary of State shall promulgate such rules and regulations with regard to the enforcement of this section as he may deem necessary to carry out its provisions. The Board shall be convened by the chairman and shall hold at least one meeting a year.

(b) Every person who engages in the business of manufacturing, exporting, or importing any arms, ammunition, or implements of war listed in a proclamation referred to in or issued under the authority of subsection (i) of this section, whether as an exporter, importer, manufacturer, or dealer, shall register with the Secretary of State his name, or business name, principal place of business, and places of business in the United States, and a list of the arms, ammunition, and implements of war which he manufactures, imports, or exports.

(c) Every person required to register under this section shall notify the Secretary of State of any change in the arms, ammunition, or implements of war which he exports, imports, or manufactures; and upon such notification the Secretary of State shall issue to such person an amended certificate of registration, free of charge, which shall remain valid until the date of expiration of the original certificate. Every person required to register under the provisions of this section shall pay a registration fee of $100. Upon receipt of the required registration fee, the Secretary of State shall issue a registration certificate valid for five years, which shall be renewable for further periods of five years upon the payment for each renewal of a fee of $100; but valid certificates of registration (including amended certificates) issued under the authority of section 2 of the joint resolution of August 31, 1935, or section 5 of the joint resolution of August 31, 1935, as amended, shall, without payment of any additional registration fee, be considered to be valid certificates of registration issued under this subsection, and shall remain valid for the same period as if this joint resolution had not been enacted.

(d) It shall be unlawful for any person to export, or attempt to export, from the United States to any other state, any arms, ammunition, or implements of war listed in a proclamation referred to in or issued under the authority of subsection (i) of this section, or to import, or attempt to import, to the United States from any other state, any of the arms, ammunition, or implements of war listed in any such proclamation, without first having submitted to the Secretary of State the name of the purchaser and the terms of sale and having obtained a license therefor.

(e) All persons required to register under this section shall maintain, subject to the inspection of the Secretary of State, or any person or persons designated by him, such permanent records of manufacture for export, importation, and exportation of arms, ammunition and implements of war as the Secretary of State shall prescribe.

(f) Licenses shall be issued by the Secretary of State to persons who have registered as herein provided for, except in cases of export or import licenses where the export of arms, ammunition, or implements of war would be in violation of this joint resolution or any other law of the United States, or of a treaty to which the United States is a party, in which cases such licenses shall not be issued; but a valid license issued under the authority of section 2 of the joint resolution of August 31, 1935, or section 5 of the joint resolution of August 31, 1935, as amended, shall be considered to be a valid license issued under this subsection, and shall remain valid for the same period as if this joint resolution had not been enacted.

(g) No purchase of arms, ammunition, or implements of war shall be made on behalf of the United States by any officer, executive department, or independent establishment of the Government from any person who shall have failed to register under the provisions of this joint resolution.

(h) The Board shall make a report to Congress on January 3 and July 3 of each year, copies of which shall be distributed as are other reports transmitted to Congress. Such reports shall contain such information and data collected by the Board as may be considered of value in the determination of questions connected with the control of trade in arms, ammunition, and implements of war, including the name of the purchaser and the terms of sale made under any such license. The Board shall include in such reports a list of all persons required to register under the provisions of this joint resolution, and full information concerning the licenses issued hereunder, including the name of the purchaser and the terms of sale made under any such license.

(i) The President is hereby authorized to proclaim upon recommendation of the Board from time to time a list of articles which shall be considered arms, ammunition, and implements of war for the purposes of this section: but the proclamation Numbered 2237, of May 1, 1937 (50 Stat. 1834), defining the term "arms, ammunition, and implements of war" shall, until it is revoked, have full force and effect as if issued under the authority of this subsection.

REGULATIONS

Section 13. The President may, from time to time, promulgate such rules and regulations, not inconsistent with law, as may be necessary and proper to carry out any of the provisions of this joint resolution; and he may exercise any power or authority conferred on him by this joint resolution through such officer or officers, or agency or agencies, as he shall direct.

UNLAWFUL USE OF THE AMERICAN FLAG

Section 14. (a) It shall be unlawful for any vessel belonging to or operating under the jurisdiction of any foreign state to use the flag of the United States thereon, or to make use of any distinctive signs or markings, indicating that the same is an American vessel.

(b) Any vessel violating the provisions of subsection (a) of this section shall be denied for a period of three months the right to enter the ports or territorial waters of the United States except in cases of force majeure.

GENERAL PENALTY PROVISION

Section 15. In every case of the violation of any of the provisions of this joint resolution or of any rule or regulation issued pursuant thereto where a specific penalty is not herein provided, such violator or violators, upon conviction, shall be fined not more than $10,000, or imprisoned not more than two years, or both.

DEFINITIONS

Section 16. For the purposes of this joint resolution—
(a) The term "United States," when used in a geographical

sense, includes the several States and Territories, the insular possessions of the United States (including the Philippine Islands), the Canal Zone, and the District of Columbia.

(b) The term "person" includes a partnership, company, association, or corporation, as well as a natural person.

(c) The term "vessel" means every description of watercraft and aircraft capable of being used as a means of transportation on, under, or over water.

(d) The term "American vessel" means any vessel documented, and any aircraft registered or licensed, under the laws of the United States.

(e) The term "state" shall include nation, government, and country.

(f) The term "citizen" shall include any individual owing allegiance to the United States, a partnership, company, or association composed in whole or in part of citizens of the United States, and any corporation organized and existing under the laws of the United States as defined in subsection (a) of this section.

SEPARABILITY OF PROVISIONS

Section 17. If any of the provisions of this joint resolution, or the application thereof to any person or circumstance, is held invalid, the remainder of the joint resolution, and the application of such provision to other persons or circumstances, shall not be affected thereby.

APPROPRIATIONS

Section 18. There is hereby authorized to be appropriated from time to time, out of any money in the Treasury not otherwise appropriated, such amounts as may be necessary to carry out the provisions and accomplish the purposes of this joint resolution.

REPEALS

Section 19. The joint resolution of August 31, 1935, as amended, and the joint resolution of January 8, 1937, are hereby repealed; but offenses committed and penalties, forfeitures, or liabilities incurred under either of such joint resolutions prior to the date of enactment of this joint resolution may be prosecuted and punished, and suits and proceedings for violations of either of such joint resolutions or of any rule or regulation issued pursuant thereto may be commenced and prosecuted, in the same manner and with the same effect as if such joint resolutions had not been repealed.

SHORT TITLE

Section 20. This joint resolution may be cited as the "Neutrality Act of 1939."

Approved, November 4, 1939.

APPENDIX C

The Declaration of Panamá

The Governments of the American Republics meeting at Panamá, have solemnly ratified their neutral status in the conflict which is disrupting the peace of Europe, but the present war may lead to unexpected results which may affect the fundamental interests of America and there can be no justification for the interests of the belligerents to prevail over the rights of neutrals causing disturbances and suffering to nations which by their neutrality in the conflict and their distance from the scene of events, should not be burdened with its fatal and painful consequences.

During the World War of 1914-1918 the Governments of Argentina, Brazil, Chile, Colombia, Ecuador and Peru advanced, or supported, individual proposals providing in principle a declaration by the American Republics that the belligerent nations must refrain from committing hostile acts within a reasonable distance from their shores.

The nature of the present conflagration, in spite of its already lamentable proportions, would not justify any obstruction to inter-American communications which, engendered by important interests, call for adequate protection. This fact requires the demarcation of a zone of security including all the normal maritime routes of communication and trade between the countries of America.

To this end it is essential as a measure of necessity to adopt immediately provisions based on the above-mentioned precedents for the safeguarding of such interests, in order to avoid a repetition of the damages and sufferings sustained by the American nations and by their citizens in the war of 1914-1918.

There is no doubt that the Governments of the American Republics must foresee those dangers and as a measure of self-protection insist that the waters to a reasonable distance from their coasts shall remain free from the commission of hostile acts or from the undertaking of belligerent activities by nations engaged in a war in which the said governments are not involved.

For these reasons the Governments of the American Republics RESOLVE AND HEREBY DECLARE:

1. As a measure of continental self-protection, the American Republics, so long as they maintain their neutrality, are as of inherent right entitled to have those waters adjacent to the American continent, which they regard as of primary concern and direct utility in their relations, free from the commission of any hostile act by any non-American belligerent nation, whether such hostile act be attempted or made from land, sea or air.

Such waters shall be defined as follows. All waters comprised within the limits set forth hereafter except the territorial waters of Canada and of the undisputed colonies and possessions of European countries within these limits:

Beginning at the terminus of the United States-Canada boundary in Passamaquoddy Bay, in 44° 46′ 36″ north latitude, and 66° 54′ 11″ west longitude;

Thence due east along the parallel 44° 46′ 36″ to a point 60° west of Greenwich;

Thence due south to a point in 20° north latitude;

Thence by a rhumb line to a point in 5° north latitude, 24° west longitude;

Thence due south to a point in 20° south latitude;

Thence by a rhumb line to a point in 58° south latitude, 57° west longitude;

Thence due west to a point in 80° west longitude;

Thence by a rhumb line to a point on the equator in 97° west longitude;

Thence by a rhumb line to a point in 15° north latitude, 120° west longitude;

Thence by a rhumb line to a point in 48° 29' 38" north latitude, 136° west longitude;

Thence due east to the Pacific terminus of the United States-Canada boundary in the Strait of Juan de Fuca.

2. The Governments of the American Republics agree that they will endeavor, through joint representation to such belligerents as may now or in the future be engaged in hostilities, to secure the compliance by them with the provisions of this Declaration, without prejudice to the exercise of the individual rights of each State inherent in their sovereignty.

3. The Governments of the American Republics further declare that whenever they consider it necessary they will consult together to determine upon the measures which they may individually or collectively undertake in order to secure the observance of the provisions of this Declaration.

4. The American Republics, during the existence of a state of war in which they themselves are not involved, may undertake, whenever they may determine that the need therefor exists, to patrol, either individually or collectively, as may be agreed upon by common consent, and in so far as the means and resources of each may permit, the waters adjacent to their coasts within the area above defined.

(Approved October 3, 1939)

INDEX

A

Airplanes, as contraband, 119-120
Alabama, case of the, 117-118
Altmark, case of the, 53-54
American States: Sixth International
  Conference of, 20
  Eighth International Conference
  of, 127
  exempted from operation of arms
  embargo, 39
American Union for Concerted
  Peace Efforts, supports Thomas
  Resolution, 42, n.29
Anna, case of the, 52
Appam, case of the, 111-112
Aquinas, St. Thomas: view on moral
  obligations of States, 8
Argentine Anti-War Treaty: com-
  mon and solidary neutral at-
  titude proposed by, 21, 126
Armed merchant ships, status of, in
  neutral ports, 58-59, 60, 67, 111-
  112
Armed Neutralities of 1780 and
  1800, 78-79
Arms and munitions of war, legality
  of sales of, 122-123
Arms embargo: Capper Resolution
  of 1929, 27
  Borah Resolution of 1932, 32-33
  applied during Chaco war, 33
  under act of 1935, 35, 124-125
    applied during Italian-Ethiopian
    war, 36-37

under act of 1936, 37-38
  applied during Spanish war, 39-40
  repeal of, urged by President, 44,
  125
  repeal of, by act of 1939, 47-48
Auxiliary transports, recommendation of Inter-American Neutrality Committee in regard to,
  119

B

Blockade: to be binding must be effective, 78ff.
  "self-blockade" imposed by Napoleon, 80
  President Madison's protest against
  pretended blockades, 81-82
  during American Civil War, 82-83
  during World War, 83-84
  extension of, to exports during
  present war, 86
Bonds and securities of belligerents,
  not purchasable under neutrality acts, 38
Borah, Senator: resolution on restatement of rules of maritime
  warfare, 19-20
  resolution on shipment of arms,
  32-33
Borchard and Lage, views of, on
  isolation and neutrality, 32, n.9
Bryan, Secretary: views of, on
  Americans traveling on belligerent merchant ships, 66-67